What Every
CHRISTIAN
Ought to Know

DAY BY DAY

Adrian Rogers

What Every
Christian
Ought to Know
Day by Day

ESSENTIAL TRUTHS FOR GROWING YOUR FAITH

PUBLISHING GROUP

NASHVILLE TENNESSEE

ISBN 978-0-8054-4800-9
B&H Publishing Group
Nashville, Tennessee
www.BHPublishingGroup.com

Dewey Decimal Classification: 230
Christian Doctrine

Printed in China
1 2 3 4 5   10 09 08

TABLE OF CONTENTS

. . . until we all reach unity in the faith and in the knowledge of God's Son, growing into a mature man with a stature measured by Christ's fullness. Then we will no longer be little children, tossed by the waves and blown around by every wind of teaching, by human cunning with cleverness in the techniques of deceit. But speaking the truth in love, let us grow in every way into Him who is the head—Christ.

— *Ephesians 4:13–15*

INTRODUCTION

The waves were enormous, much bigger than those in my native state of Florida. We were in Maui, Hawaii, and I was excited. I love to bodysurf. Catch a wave just right, and you can ride without a board all the way to the beach.

I worked my way out to where the waves were breaking. I saw my wave building up. This was going to be a great ride, I could tell. But I knew I had to catch it just right. At that special moment, I put my head down and gave a kick. That's when the action really began.

The monster wave (you may have guessed) didn't take me to the beach. Instead, it picked me up like a rag doll and body-slammed me to the ocean floor. The lights went out. I was numb. "Let me check. Can I move my legs? My arms?" Nothing appeared broken. I made my way carefully to the shore.

When I got back on solid ground, I turned to see the big sign posted: "No Bodysurfing: Spinal Injury May

Result." The warning was right there—in plain sight—but I had been saturated with ignorance.

So much for the old proverb, "What you don't know can't hurt you."

In much the same way, I believe that there are some basic truths every Christian ought to know. Many people founder in a sea of moral relativism and vague religious opinions. Our society boasts about *pluralism*—which means there is room for every idea—but actually, we practice *syncretism* by blending all religious thought into a bland mixture of spiritual pablum. Americans love to prate about values but are quickly intimidated when the question is asked, "*Whose* values?" It is more morality by majority than by true, biblical virtues.

Our generation has substituted facts for truth. We don't ask, "Is it true?" We just want to know, "Does it work?" And yet the Bible exhorts us, "Buy the truth, and do not sell it" (Prov. 23:23 NKJV).

- We must *prize* the truth.
- We must *purchase* the truth.
- We must *preserve* the truth.

Salvation is free, but the quest for truth is costly. Yet while discipleship requires great effort, ignorance is far more devastating. The quest for truth will cost precious time, but it is worth it. I am sure that the year we spend together in these pages will result in rich dividends of blessing, direction, and protection.

This book deals with fundamental truth that *Every Christian Ought to Know*. It is written to be clear but not simplistic. It is for the new believer but also for those who seem bogged down in their Christian walk.

May we learn how to live for Him *Day by Day*.

January

The Bible Is the Word of God

Every word of God is pure;
He is a shield to those who take refuge in Him.

Proverbs 30:5

"Man has only three problems," I once said to a lawyer seated next to me on an airplane. "They are: sin, sorrow, and death." He said, "No, there are more problems than that."

"All right, tell me a fourth one." He thought for a minute and said, "Man has only three problems." Indeed, every other problem in the world is just a subset of sin, sorrow, and death.

And the Bible is the only book on Earth that has the answer to all three conditions. For this reason, it is important to have a rock-ribbed assurance that the Bible is the Word of God.

The grass withers, and the flower drops off,
but the word of the Lord endures forever.
1 Peter 1:24–25

Some despise the Bible, while others merely deny it. Still others distort it and have warped, misused, and abused it. But even though many actively oppose this book, I believe the greatest enemy of the Word of God is the so-called Christian who simply ignores the Bible or disregards it. He gives only lip service to it.

As someone has said, "These hath God married and no man shall part: dust in the Bible and drought in the heart." The things that keep us going are truth and conviction—the things we know are true. Feelings come and go, but God's Word never wavers.

It is easier for heaven and earth to pass away than for one stroke of a letter in the law to drop out.
Luke 16:17

Your salvation depends on understanding the gospel message of the Bible.

Your assurance depends on resting in the truth of the Bible.

Your spiritual growth depends on living by the principles of the Bible.

And your power in being a witness depends on the confidence you have in the Bible.

Therefore, you must be absolutely certain that the Bible is the Word of God.

It is not as though the word of God has failed.
Romans 9:6

It is commonly assumed that there must be scientific errors in the Bible. Before you say that, however, you should make certain you know two things: both *science* and *the Bible.*

Most often, those who claim that there are scientific errors in the Bible do not clearly understand either subject. And those who *do* have a good, realistic understanding of science would admit that science itself is in a continual state of flux, constantly changing.

Not so the Bible. Its scientific accuracy, in fact, confirms it as the Word of God.

God is not a man who lies,
or a son of man who changes His mind.
Numbers 23:19

The accepted science of yesterday is not necessarily the science of today. It has been estimated that the library in the Louvre in Paris has three and a half miles of books on science. Most every one of them is obsolete.

In 1861, the French Academy of Science wrote a pamphlet stating that there were fifty-one incontrovertible scientific facts that proved the Bible was not true. Today, however, there is not a respected scientist in the world who would accept or agree to even one of those so-called "facts." Science is ever changing, but God's Word does not change.

He stretches the northern skies over empty space;
He hangs the earth on nothing.
Job 26:7

Ancient cultures did not always know that the Earth was suspended in space. The ancient Egyptians believed it was supported by pillars. The ancient Greeks thought it was carried by Atlas. The Hindus held that it was resting on the backs of gigantic elephants, who were standing on a tortoise, who was standing on a coiled serpent swimming in a cosmic sea.

So how did Job—whose book that bears his name is perhaps the oldest piece of literature known to man—understand that the Earth is hanging "on nothing"? He could only have known through divine inspiration.

God is enthroned above the circle of the earth.
Isaiah 40:22

Another scientific fact we take quite for granted is that the Earth is round. Do we know this by natural observation? Not at all. But we've seen pictures from outer space, so we know beyond a doubt that the Earth is round. Even as late as 1492, however, when "Columbus sailed the ocean blue," people did not know this. They warned him to be careful, fearing that he might sail off the edge of the Earth on his travels.

Yet Isaiah, in 750 BC, talked about the "circle" of the Earth, using a Hebrew word meaning "globe" or "sphere." Long before man knew it scientifically, God had already revealed it.

JANUARY 8

Darkness and light are alike to You.
Psalm 139:12

The Bible teaches that when Jesus comes again, it will be both daylight and dark at the same time. He said, for example, "I tell you, on that night two will be in one bed . . . two women will be grinding grain together . . . two will be in a field: one will be taken, and the other will be left" (Luke 17:34–36).

This seems contradictory—some in bed, some at work. But while it will be light on one side of the globe, it will be dark on the other side when Jesus Christ comes again. Of course, this did not take by surprise the One who created the world. He knew it from the very beginning.

Look at the sky and count the stars,
if you are able to count them.
Genesis 15:5

More than a hundred years before Christ, the leading astronomer and scientist of the day—Hipparchus—laid down his pen, rubbed his eyes, and declared that he had counted the stars. There were 1,022 of them, he said. It wasn't until 250 years later that Ptolemy upgraded the count to 1,056.

But 1,300 years later, Galileo invented his first crude telescope, turned it up to the heavens, and looked beyond the stars that could be seen with the naked eye. On that day he learned what God had been saying all along. No fool would ever try to count the stars.

The hosts of heaven cannot be counted;
the sand of the sea cannot be measured.

Jeremiah 33:22

I remember reading in a scientific journal that scientists were trying to understand the size of the universe. The journal stated that there are more suns like our sun in the known universe than there are grains of sand on all the seashores of the Earth.

I'm from West Palm Beach, Florida, and I can't imagine counting the grains of sand in just a city block! And yet, there are more suns in our universe than grains of sand throughout the Earth! Think again of Hipparchus—one, two, three—1,022 stars. He could have saved some time had he turned to the Word of God.

The life of every creature is its blood.
Leviticus 17:14

A little known fact is how George Washington, the father of our country, died. He was sick, so the physicians bled him. When he didn't get well, they bled him again. When he still didn't get well, they bled him a third time. Without realizing it, they bled him to death! (Could it be that ever since, the politicians have been bleeding *us* to death to get even?)

Today, rather than removing what they thought to be his "bad blood," they might have given him a blood transfusion. That would have been in keeping with what God had said long before: "The life of every creature is its blood."

For the Lord gives wisdom; from His mouth come knowledge and understanding.

Proverbs 2:6

The ancient Egyptians were clever and skilled, yet they had some foolish ideas. They thought, for example, that if you wanted to prevent your hair from turning gray, you should anoint it with the blood of a black cat that had been boiled in oil or with the fat of a rattlesnake.

We are still trying to understand some of the things the Egyptians knew about embalming and a variety of other things. They were highly intelligent people. Moses, we know, was said to be schooled in all the wisdom of the Egyptians. I'm glad, though, when I look in the Bible, I don't find any such absurd medical treatments.

As long as he has the infection; he is unclean.
He must live alone in a place outside the camp.

Leviticus 13:46

During what came to be known as the "black plague" of the fourteenth century, one out of every four people in Europe died. They didn't know what to do with it. They couldn't control it. They had no concept of microbiology like we have now. Do you know what finally brought the plague to an end? The Bible! They learned to quarantine from the Word of God.

I have only touched the surface over the past few days of the many medical and scientific truths contained in the Bible. Frankly, I'm glad the Bible and modern science don't always agree. Science changes. The Bible—never!

I meditate on all You have done;
I reflect on the work of Your hands.
Psalm 143:5

Although I've mentioned several areas of science where the Bible has been vindicated, the Bible is not primarily a science book. It is not written to tell us how the heavens go; it is written to tell us how to go to heaven. Similarly, although the Bible contains accurate historical information, it is not primarily a history book. It is "His story," the story of God.

If a historian or scientist has a good word to say about the Bible, it shouldn't give you any more faith in the Bible, just a little more faith in the scientist or the historian. The Bible has and will stand the test of time.

The Lord then said to Moses,
"Write this down on a scroll as a reminder."
Exodus 17:14

Some scholars have long ridiculed the idea that Moses wrote the first five books of the Bible. They claim that men didn't even know how to write in Moses' time.

But one day in northern Egypt, a lady was spading her garden when she came across some clay tablets, written from people in Egypt to people in Palestine (the Holy Land) centuries before Moses was born. Not only did these ancient cultures know how to write, they also had a postal service that allowed them to send correspondence back and forth to one another. Don't count Moses out so easily!

*God has numbered the days of your kingdom
and brought it to an end.*
Daniel 5:26

Remember the handwriting on the wall which Daniel interpreted to say that Babylon would fall during Belshazzar's reign? Scholars have laughed at this, claiming they had records that said the last king of Babylon was Nabonitus.

But more recent findings have revealed that Nabonitus and Belshazzar were father and son who ruled together, making them both kings at the same time! This also helps us understand why Daniel was offered the "third highest position" in the kingdom if he could read the handwriting (Dan. 5:16). Just give people time, and they start to catch up with the Bible.

For God is not the author of confusion.
1 Corinthians 14:33 (KJV)

The Bible is a library of sixty-six books written by at least forty authors, perhaps more. These people lived in a period of time spanning at least 1,600 years, in about thirteen different countries, on three different continents. They came from all backgrounds: shepherds, kings, soldiers, princes, fishermen, scholars, historians, professional men, common laborers. The Bible is written in different styles and in at least three different languages.

And yet when you bring all of that together, it makes one book that has one story. Only God could create that kind of unity.

I urge you, brothers . . . that you be united with the same understanding and the same conviction.
1 Corinthians 1:10

The Bible has *one theme*—redemption.
The Bible has *one hero*—the Lord Jesus.
The Bible has *one villain*—the devil.
The Bible has *one purpose*—the glory of God.

All of its parts fit together. Can you imagine taking forty different people over a period of 1,600 years from many different countries and occupations, telling them each to write inde pendently of one another without having read what the others had written? Put that all together and see what kind of hodgepodge you would have! Yet we have this wonderful unity in the Word of God.

*Join them together into a single stick
so that they become one in your hand.*
Ezekiel 37:17

Suppose they decided to build a monument using stones gathered from all fifty states—coral stone from Florida, granite from Georgia, lime stone from Indiana, sandstone from Nevada. Different colors, cut in different shapes. Work men uncrate the stones to begin putting them together—and all the pieces interlock! There is not one stone too many, not one stone too few. Nothing needs to be built up or shaved down.

Would you say this happened by chance? No, there would have to have been a master archi tect who designed the monument and sent his instructions to the various quarries. True?

All Scripture is inspired by God.
2 Timothy 3:16

When we get this Book written over a period of 1,600 years, employing forty different authors from all walks of life writing in three different languages, it comes together to make one beautiful temple of God's truth. Nothing needs to be added or taken away or embellished. There it stands—one Book!

We can't say that it just happened. No thinking person would honestly say it was an accident. No! The unity of the Bible is one of the most wonderful proofs of the inspiration of God's Word—that all Scripture is given by inspiration of God.

No prophecy ever came by the will of man . . .
moved by the Holy Spirit, men spoke from God.
2 Peter 1:21

Another great proof for the inspiration of the Bible is the fulfilled prophecy it contains. This Book has predictions of things that have yet to happen and *will* happen, established by the fact that it includes predictions of so many things that already *have* happened.

It has been wisely said that you can take a child of God, put him in a dungeon with a Bible and a candle and lock him away, and he will know more about what's going on in today's world than all the pundits in Washington. It's amazing to see history fit into the sockets of prophecy and actually fulfill it.

One will come from you to be ruler over Israel
for Me. His origin is from antiquity.
Micah 5:2

Think about the prophecies that were realized in the Lord Jesus alone. Scholars say He fulfilled more than 300 Old Testament prophecies. His enemies will say, "Oh sure, He fulfilled all these prophecies because He rigged it!"

Well, for the next several days, let's look at some of these things that He "arranged." First, He arranged to be born in Bethlehem. Could you arrange where you were going to be born? Then he arranged for Isaiah to record details about His life 700 years before He was born (Isaiah 9 and 53). Did you arrange to have the history of your life written before you were born?

A gang of evildoers has closed in on me;
they pierced my hands and my feet.

Psalm 22:16

Did you know if you read Psalm 22, composed by David centuries before Jesus was born, you will read a description of the crucifixion of Jesus Christ, written from the viewpoint of a man standing at the foot of the cross? It tells about the piercing of His hands and feet, the gambling for His garments, even the very words that Jesus would say while He hung there.

When Jesus spoke these words from the cross, He wasn't looking back and quoting David. Rather, David was writing as someone who was a mystical eyewitness to Christ's crucifixion, looking forward and quoting Jesus. Amazing!

I will put My words in his mouth, and he will
tell them everything I command him.
Deuteronomy 18:18

When David wrote his prophecies about Christ 1,000 years beforehand, the common form of capital punishment used by the Jews was stoning. The Romans—the ones who would use crucifixion as their preferred form of execution—had not even come into power yet.

More than this, the Bible told us ahead of time that Jesus would be crucified between two thieves (Isaiah 53:9–12) and that Judas would betray Him for exactly thirty pieces of silver (Zechariah 11:12). Such precise details were not left to chance or unforeseen. They were already spelled out in black and white.

*All this has happened so that the prophetic
Scriptures would be fulfilled.*
Matthew 26:56

The most telling "arrangement" Jesus set into motion was to arise from the dead and be seen by more than 500 witnesses. Some say the disciples were merely hallucinating. What? Five hundred of them hallucinating at the same time? Having the same hallucination?

Furthermore, nobody would willingly die for a lie if he knew it was a lie. Yet the early followers of Christ laid down their lives for the faith, even though most of these prophecies were not fulfilled by Jesus' friends but by His enemies, those who had the most to lose by their coming true. This proves the inspiration of the Bible.

Heaven and earth will pass away,
but My words will never pass away.
Luke 21:33

The Bible is not the Book of the Month. It is the Book of the Ages. There is no book that has had as much opposition as the Bible. Men have laughed at it; they have scorned it; they have ridiculed it; they have made laws against it. There was a time in Scottish history when to own a Bible was a crime worthy of death. There are those who have vowed and declared that they will destroy this Book.

But no matter how people rant and rave, we are all like blades of grass before the unchanging words of Scripture. We are going to wither and die, but God's Word stands forever!

My words that I have put in your mouth
will not depart from your mouth.
Isaiah 59:21

We have some theological experts who think they have been called upon to re-examine the Bible. (As far as I'm concerned, we ought to re-examine *them,* because the Word of the Lord endures forever!)

The Bible is to judge us; we are not to judge the Bible. If you throw the old Book into the fiery furnace, it will emerge without even the smell of smoke on its clothes.

Here we are in a new and modern age, and we are still studying this old, old Book. It has stood the test of time, towering over all other books.

For the word of God is quick, and powerful,
and sharper than any two-edged sword.
Hebrews 4:12 *(KJV)*

The word "quick" in the verse above is the same word from which we get our word "zoo" and "zoology." It means the Word of God is alive, that it pulsates with life and power.

The word "powerful" is the Greek word *energes*, the word we get "energy" from. Truly, there is life and energy in the Bible. We read other books, but this Book reads us.

It is incredible! It is saving to the sinner and continually refreshing to the saved. I have used this Book many, many times to lead people to Christ and have seen them transformed by it.

*Is not My word like fire . . . and like
a sledgehammer that pulverizes rock?*
Jeremiah 23:29

When Billy Graham came to London to preach
in 1954, a great crowd gathered, including two
men who were sitting together, finding fault
with the flamboyant American evangelist. Yet
when Billy began to preach, one of them said
to the other, "I don't know about you, but I'm
going down there to give my heart to Christ."
The man next to him said, "I'll go with you.
And here's your billfold. I'm a pickpocket."

Rev. Graham once said, "I found in my preaching that the Word of God was like a rapier, and
when I quoted it under the inspiration of the
Spirit, I could slay everything before me."

How sweet Your word is to my taste—
sweeter than honey to my mouth.
Psalm 119:103

The Word of God has the power (as the old hymn says) to "rescue the perishing" and "care for the dying" and "snatch them in pity from sin and the grave." I know personally the transforming power of the Word of God. He has changed my life through it!

It is saving for the sinner. The Scriptures are able to stir the conscience, convict the mind, and convert the soul.

It is sweet for the saint. So many times I have found treasure and peace in the Bible. Oh, how precious are the words of God!

Let your hands be strong, you who now hear these words that the prophets spoke.
Zechariah 8:9

You can trust the Bible. You will never be all you want to be in Christ until you come to the firm, unshakable conviction that the Bible is the Word of God.

It is sufficient for the sufferer. How many times have people pillowed their head on the precious promises of the Word of God? I feel sorry for those who do not have a Bible to lean on.

It is satisfying to the scholar. It is so deep that we can swim in it and never touch bottom, and yet so precious that a little child can come and drink from it without fear of drowning.

FEBRUARY

THE ASSURANCE
OF SALVATION

I have written these things to you . . . so that you may know that you have eternal life.
1 John 5:13

One basic thing all Christians should know beyond the shadow of any doubt is that they are saved—that all of their sins are forgiven and buried in the grave of God's forgetfulness, that Jesus Christ has come to live in them, and that they are bound for heaven, either when they die or the Lord returns.

It is much better to be a shouting Christian than a doubting Christian. We ought not to walk around like a question mark with our heads bent over, but like an exclamation point! We should not be saying, "I hope I'm saved," but "*I know* I'm saved!"

Let us draw near with a true heart
in full assurance of faith.
Hebrews 10:22

I was making a ministry call in the hospital with a lady who was dying. I had been called to her bedside to pray with her.

I asked her if she was assured of salvation. She answered, "No." I asked her if she wanted to be saved. She said, "Indeed, I do." So I explained to her from the Word of God how to be saved, and I led her as she asked Jesus Christ to forgive her sins and come into her heart. Here was a precious lady who in just a little while would be going into the presence of God, and now she had the blessed assurance of being welcomed there—an assurance each of us can enjoy.

*Our gospel did not come to you in word only, but
also in power . . . and with much assurance.*

1 Thessalonians 1:5

Someone has well said, "If you could have
salvation and not know it, you could lose it and
not miss it." Yes, if you have genuine salvation,
you should know it. And if it is real, thank God
you can never lose it. We ought to have abso
lute certainty about things like this.

When we talk about the assurance of salvation,
we are talking about something of vital impor
tance. We are not talking about denominational
preference, the height of the church steeple, or
the color of the carpet. We are talking about
the eternal destiny of your soul, the knowledge
that you are heaven born and heaven bound.

Have mercy on some who doubt.
Jude 22

Is it possible to be saved and to have doubts about it? Certainly. Doubt doesn't necessarily mean that you haven't been saved. As a matter of fact, we only tend to doubt that which we believe. Doubt is to your spirit what pain is to your body. Pain doesn't mean that one is dead. It means that there is life, but that something is wrong, that a part of the body is not functioning as it ought.

Yes, doubt is possible, but not profitable. I have never known any Christian who was really effective in his or her service to the Lord who did not have the full assurance of salvation.

"Lord," Thomas said, "we don't know where You're going. How can we know the way?"
John 14:5

One lady told an evangelist, "I have been saved for twenty-five years and never had a doubt." He said, "I doubt you have been saved." Perhaps he's right. It would be like saying, 'We have been married for twenty-five years and never had an argument."

Indeed, we may have doubts, and we may have arguments, but neither one is good for us. They may be facts of life, but we must guard against them. Trying to live the Christian life with doubts is much like driving an automobile with the brakes on. You need to have not a hope-so, think-so, maybe-so, but a know-so salvation.

Unless someone is born of water and the Spirit,
he cannot enter the kingdom of God.

John 3:5

Being born spiritually is much like being born physically. One reason why birth makes such a perfect example of salvation is because all of us have experienced a physical birth and can relate to the facts about it.

For example, in birth a conception takes place. Jesus said that we are born of water and the Spirit in order to enter the kingdom of God. Water speaks of the Word of God, and the Spirit means the Spirit of God. When these come together in the womb of faith, a wonderful conception occurs. We are born again, and our life is held forever in His hands.

*Whatever is born of the flesh is flesh,
and whatever is born of the Spirit is spirit.*

John 3:6

Parents do not manufacture babies in the true sense of the word. They merely pass on the life that has been given to them. Likewise in the new birth, the life of God is transmitted into us. Salvation is not only getting man out of earth into heaven, but getting God out of heaven into man through His Spirit.

And just as we receive the nature of our fleshly parents, we receive from God a new character. Christians are not just nice people; they are new creatures. We are not like a tadpole that has become a frog, but like a frog that has become a prince through the kiss of grace.

*You will be established
on a foundation of righteousness.*
Isaiah 54:14

Just as a birth is a once-for-all experience in the natural realm, so it is in the spiritual realm. When a baby is born in earthly society, a record is written down. And when a child of God is born again, a new name is written down in glory. This speaks of a completed fact.

It is important that we understand this, because no one can ever be unborn. Even when one's body ceases to exist, the spirit of an individual goes on timeless, dateless, and measureless into eternity. A birth is a starting place. A little child is all tomorrows. And when we come to Jesus, we are not yesterdays—we are all tomorrows.

Everyone who believes that
Jesus is the Messiah has been born of God.
1 John 5:1

A birth is a definite experience. It would be almost nonsensical for me to ask, "Have you ever been born?" But suppose I did ask it, and you were to answer, "I hope so. I'm doing the best I can." Or, "I have always been born." No, birth implies a certainty. There was a time when you were not born and a time when you were.

The story is told of Will Rogers who one time went in to get a passport, and the official said, "We need your birth certificate." He asked, "What for?" They said, "For proof of your birth." He shot back, "Well, here I am, ain't I?" Truly, if you are trusting Jesus, you are saved.

For by grace you are saved through faith,
and this is not from yourselves; it is God's gift.

Ephesians 2:8

Many people think God is like Santa Claus—making a list, checking it twice, trying to see who's naughty and nice. They think that one day at the judgment, we will stand before Him where He will weigh the good against the bad and see which side the balance comes down on. Most people honestly believe they can behave themselves into heaven.

But look carefully at the Scripture verse above. Salvation is not of ourselves. It is not of works. The devil will encourage you to believe, "It is grace *plus* what I do. I do my part and God does His." No, our salvation is of God alone.

*We conclude that a man is justified
by faith apart from works of law.*

Romans 3:28

I've heard this illustration used by those who believe in works plus grace: If you were rowing across a stream in a rowboat and pulled on one oar—we will call it "works"—you would go in a circle. If you pulled only on the other oar—"faith"—your circle would then go in the other direction. But if you pulled on both oars at the same time, only then would you go across the stream successfully.

This may sound like a good illustration, but it has a fatal flaw: *we are not going to heaven in a rowboat!* We are going to heaven by the grace of God. It is not of self, and it is not of works.

For your sake He became poor, so that
by His poverty you might become rich.
2 Corinthians 8:9

Grace is the characteristic of God's nature that makes Him love sinners. He does not love us because we're valuable; we are valuable because He loves us. This is sheer grace—something we do not deserve at all. It is God's unmerited love and favor shown to sinners who deserve judgment instead.

When you think of grace, think of Jesus dying in agony and blood upon the cross for undeserving sinners. We have nothing to commend us to God. We are sinners by birth, by choice, and by practice, yet God loves us in spite of our sin. That is grace.

The grace of our Lord overflowed, along with the faith and love that are in Christ Jesus.
1 Timothy 1:14

Faith means forsaking dependence on all your good intentions, your good deeds, and your so-called sense of self-worth. You turn your back on sin and trust God, placing your faith where He has put your sins—on the Lord Jesus.

Think of grace as Christ's nail-pierced hand reaching down from heaven as He says, "I love you. I want to save you." Think of faith as your sin-stained hand reaching up to Him as you say, "God, I need You. I want You." And when you put your hand of faith into God's hand of grace, that is salvation. It is not faith that saves; it is grace that saves. Faith lays hold of grace.

The tablets were the work of God,
and the writing was God's writing.
Exodus 32:16

Suppose you have a friend who drives up in front of your house with a $50,000 automobile that he wants to give you. But you say, "I can't let you do this. Here's a quarter. Let me at least contribute something to it." So he actually pays $49,999.75 for the car.

Later, when you are out driving, someone says, "My, that's a nice car you've got there." You say, "Yes, my friend and I bought it." That would be a little unfair to your friend, wouldn't it? We must remember that we cannot take any praise or credit for our salvation. There will be no peacocks strutting around in heaven.

The one who says, "I have come to know Him,"
without keeping His commands, is a liar.
1 John 2:4

John does not beat around the bush here. He says in effect, "Look, don't tell me you are saved if you are not keeping God's commandments. If you say you are, you are a liar."

Let me be clear. We have learned already that salvation is not of works. You are not saved because you keep the commandments, but you will keep the commandments if you are saved! This is one of the birthmarks of the believer— one of those pieces of evidence that are traits of the twice born. Obedience is not something that has the power to save you, but it is a way to test your salvation.

Jesus answered, "If anyone loves Me,
he will keep My word."
John 14:23

Early sailors did not have global positioning
satellites and radio signals to guide them, yet
they sailed over the trackless seas by keeping
their eyes on the heavens. They called this
"keeping the stars."

Keeping the stars is a whole lot like keeping the
commandments. It doesn't mean sinless perfec
tion. Any sailor could occasionally get blown
off course, become distracted, and waver this
way and that. Yet when our heart's desire is to
keep God's Word, He steers us in the right
direction. From the moment I gave my heart to
Jesus, I have had a desire to keep His Word.

Everyone who has been born of God does not sin, because His seed remains in him.

1 John 3:9

You may say, "I'm not sure I'm saved, because I know that the ability to sin is still within me." The word John used for "sin" in this verse is in the present tense, meaning a habitual course of action. John was saying that a person who is born of God does not make sin his practice, his lifestyle, his habit. It doesn't mean that he never, ever slips into sin.

Before I was saved, I was running *to* sin. Since being saved, I am running *from* it. I may fall, I may slip, I may fail, but my heart's desire is to live for God. If that is your testimony as well, you can be assured of your salvation.

By this all people will know that you are My disciples, if you have love for one another.

John 13:35

Remember that when we believe on the Lord Jesus Christ, we are born of God. We have a new nature—God's nature. This places us in the family of God, having brothers and sisters.

So if we are born of God and have become partakers of His divine nature, love will auto matically be in our heart, because God is love.

To be God's child is to share God's nature. We don't need a bumper sticker or a lapel pin to prove that we are Christians. Love is the very nature of God, and therefore it is characteristic of His children.

*We know that we have passed from death to life
because we love our brothers.*
1 John 3:14

If God's love is in us, we are going to love what
He loves. This includes loving His dear family.
That's why it is foolish to say yes to Jesus and
no to His church.

The church is a *building*. And Jesus Christ is its
foundation. Who could say yes to the founda
tion and no to the building that rests upon it?

The church is His *bride*. Who could say yes to
the groom and no to the bride?

The church is His *body*. Who could say yes to
Christ—its head—and no to the body?

*The person who does not love his brother whom he
has seen cannot love God whom he has not seen.*

1 John 4:20

One of the marks of the twice born is that we
love one another—the members of His church.
This doesn't mean, however, that all of us are
lovable by nature. In fact, we are all sinners. A
church is comprised of people who have finally
realized that they are sinners and have banded
themselves together to do something about it.

This makes the church the only organization I
know of, besides Hell's Angels, in which you
have to profess to be bad before you can join.
And yet we Christians are called to love the
church—to love those who, like us, are sinners
who have turned our lives over to Jesus.

Whatever you did for one of the least
of these brothers of Mine, you did for Me.
Matthew 25:40

A man named Saul, who later became the apostle Paul, was on the road to Damascus to arrest Christians. The Lord Jesus appeared to him in a blinding light and said, "Saul, Saul, why are you persecuting Me?"

Saul could have answered back, "Whoever you are, I am not persecuting you; I am persecuting the church." The truth is, however, that when one persecutes the church, he is in reality persecuting Jesus Christ Himself.

To neglect the church is to neglect Jesus, and to love the church is to love Him.

*The one who believes in the Son of God
has the testimony in himself.*
1 John 5:10

Truly, this is the greatest and strongest test of our salvation. All of the others grow out of it. Biblical belief (or confidence) is not just an intellectual exercise. You do not believe *about* Jesus; you believe *in* Jesus. You can believe an airplane can fly, but you don't really show your trust in it until you get on board.

Again, I remind you that salvation is more than an intellectual ascent to biblical facts. It requires our belief in Jesus. Notice, too, that this verse is cast in the present tense. It doesn't talk about "the one who *has* believed" but "the one who believes." Our confidence is here and now.

*Believe on the Lord Jesus,
and you will be saved.*

Acts 16:31

Sometimes, a person will say, "Yes, I am saved. I remember walking down the aisle when I was nine years old, greeting the pastor, and giving my heart to Jesus. I may not be living for God right now, but . . ."

Many people want to go back to an event from the past. Some even say, "If you cannot show me the place and tell me the moment when you received Jesus, then you are not saved." But this is not biblical and is not so. The Bible never says that you will know you are saved by something you recall in the past. If you are believing now, then you did believe.

*May the God of hope fill you with
all joy and peace in believing.*
Romans 15:13

Some true believers are concerned because they can't remember the exact time of their conversion the way others can. Some had a cataclysmic experience when they turned to faith in Christ. Others grew up in a Christian family and were nurtured along until one day it dawned on them that they were trusting Jesus as their personal Lord and Savior.

But that doesn't mean they were half saved, and then three-quarters saved, and then all the way saved. No one is half saved. To be half saved is to be altogether lost. The only question is, "Are you believing in Christ right now?"

Now this is His command: that we believe
in the name of His Son Jesus Christ.
1 John 3:23

Suppose we were both traveling from Orlando, Florida, to Atlanta, Georgia. You were driving, and I was flying. Since you were traveling where the road was clearly marked, you were easily able to recognize the moment you crossed the state line. But from the air, I couldn't be sure of the exact moment when the plane crossed over from Florida into Georgia. Yet here we would sit—both of us, in Atlanta. Obviously at some point, I crossed the state line.

I tell you, if you *are* trusting Jesus, you *did* trust Jesus. The real test is not remembering that you did, but knowing that you are.

The Spirit Himself testifies together with our spirit that we are God's children.

Romans 8:16

The witness of the Holy Spirit in our hearts is not an emotional feeling. Your emotions are located at the shallowest part of your nature, but salvation is indeed the deepest work of God. He will not do the deepest work in the shallowest part.

The witness of the Spirit is the Holy Spirit's speaking to your human spirit with a quiet confidence that you belong to Jesus Christ. It is an inner awareness that helps those who are saved know that they are. A true believer with this witness in his heart is never at the mercy of an unbeliever who has an argument.

*Anyone who hears My word and
believes Him who sent Me has eternal life.*
John 5:24

One night while out witnessing, I asked a man
if he wanted to receive Jesus Christ as his Lord
and Savior. He said he did. And after we prayed
together, I said to him, "I want to give you your
spiritual birth certificate." I read him the verse
above in its entirety.

I then asked, "Do you now have eternal life?"
He said, "I hope so." We went around and
around about this. I would re-read this verse,
then ask him, "Do you have eternal life?" Again
and again, he would say, "I hope so." Finally,
the light came on and he realized, "Yes! I do
have eternal life." He had God's Word on it.

Everyone who calls on the name
of the Lord will be saved.
Romans 10:13

If you have never received Jesus Christ as your personal Lord and Savior, you may do so right now. By an act of faith, trust Him to save you. He is ready and willing, and He will do it this very moment. Don't look for a sign. Don't ask for a feeling. Stand on His Word.

If you are saved and yet you still have doubts, don't look back to some past experience to try to confirm your salvation. Ask yourself: "Am I trusting Jesus?" If not, trust Him right now. If you are, then you will have a desire to obey His Word and to love His people. You will have a quiet confidence that you belong to Him.

I have trusted in Your faithful love;
my heart will rejoice in Your deliverance.

Psalm 13:5

As a young teen, I gave my heart to Christ. But for some months, I was up and down. I didn't know whether I was lost or saved. One night after walking my girlfriend home, I remember stopping at a street corner, wanting to get this settled. I looked up into the starry sky and prayed, wanting to look into the face of God.

"O Lord," I said, "I pray with all my heart, trusting You to save me. If I was saved before, this can't take it away. But if I wasn't, I am driving a peg down tonight. This settles it forever." A river of peace started to flow in my heart, which has continued to flow my entire life.

March

Eternal Security

*I give them eternal life, and they
will never perish—ever!*
John 10:28

Is there anything better than being saved? Be careful how you answer, now, because this is a loaded question. Yes, there's something better than being saved—it's being saved and *knowing* you're saved, having the blessed assurance we talked about during the last month.

But is there anything better than being saved and knowing you're saved? Yes, there is! It is being saved, knowing that you're saved, and knowing that you can never ever lose your salvation. This doctrine of "eternal security" is not incidental but is absolutely essential to your Christian life.

Walk worthy of the calling you have received.
Ephesians 4:1

Can you imagine a little child in a family who doesn't know from one day to the next whether he may be in the family? Perhaps one day he was naughty and disobeyed, so he's no longer a member of the family. Then after several weeks he repents, and he is received back in. Then after a little while, he's out of the family again. Can you imagine what an emotional wreck this child would be?

I know Christians who are emotional wrecks because they don't have the assurance that they are children of God. They feel like they're in, then they're out. It doesn't have to be that way.

*This is the promise that He
Himself made to us: eternal life.*
1 John 2:25

In 1937, as the Golden Gate Bridge began to rise hundreds of feet above the icy, swirling waters of San Francisco Bay, the workmen were afraid for their lives. Some of them fell and drowned—twenty-three in all. So management decided to build a safety net underneath the workers at a cost of $100,000. But it ended up being a great saving, because the work went 25 percent faster and only ten more men fell from the bridge—each of them into the safety net.

Why could these people work with so much more productivity? Because of their security! And that's the way it is in the Christian life.

*Don't work for the food that perishes
but for the food that lasts for eternal life.*
John 6:27

When you know you're saved, you can be more productive, offering grateful service. And when you are confident of the future, you can more easily concentrate on the present.

A lot of people would like to be saved, but they think, "Well, I just can't live it. I can't hold out. I know how weak I am." They're afraid that they could walk forward in the church, profess to be a Christian, and then fall away and look foolish. How wonderful to tell these people that the God who saves them is the God who will keep them. It's thrilling to assure people that they can be safe for all eternity.

Therefore don't judge anything prematurely,
before the Lord comes.
1 Corinthians 4:5

By eternal security, we don't mean that once a person joins a church and gets baptized, she's eternally secure. No, we're talking about some one who has become a partaker of the divine nature, a person who has been reborn, a person who has genuinely become a child of God.

Sometimes when I teach on this subject of the new birth, a person will say, "I know somebody who used to be a Christian who is no longer a Christian." I say, "Well, you *think* you know someone who used to be a Christian. Maybe she never was a Christian. Maybe she still is. We are not equipped to judge that."

On that day many will say to Me, "Lord, Lord, didn't we prophesy in Your name?"
Matthew 7:22

Many people look like Christians and act like Christians, but they've never been saved. In the verse above, the word "prophesy" means speaking for God; so evidently, these were preachers. They claimed that they were genuine followers, the way people claim today that they are good Christians because they sing in the choir, take up the offering, or teach Sunday school. But Jesus says to them, "I never knew you!"

He didn't say, "You had it, but you lost it." He says instead, "I never knew you!" This person didn't lose his salvation. According to Jesus, he never had it.

If they had belonged to us,
they would have remained with us.
1 John 2:19

This verse talks about those who begin for a while and then walk away from the faith. These people start out for God, continue for a season, and then go back to the old way.

Someone might say, "They lost their salvation." But John says, "No, they walked away from us because they were not really of us. Had they truly been one of us, they would no doubt have continued on with us."

Here's a saying I like that sums it up: "The faith that fizzles before the finish had a flaw from the first." They never really knew the Lord.

Who can separate us from the love of Christ?
Romans 8:35

Romans 8:38–39 is a sacred promise from God to you. I ask that you get your Bible and read it right now. It tells of several strong opponents that can never separate us from God's love.

• Death. Life. Angels. Rulers. Powers.

• Things present. Things to come.

• Height. Depth. Or any other created thing.

I challenge you to name any other force that has the power to separate us from the love of God, other than the ones Paul mentioned.

We love because He first loved us.
1 John 4:19

Salvation is the work of God. It is not "do-it-yourself." Do you think you were convicted of sin by yourself? The Bible says, "There is no one who seeks God" (Rom. 3:11). God Himself is the One who ran you down and convicted you of your sin. If He couldn't run faster than you could, you would never have been saved.

Not only is He the Convictor, He is also the Convertor. He is the One who opened your understanding. That's the reason I pray about this before I preach, because anything I can talk you into, someone else can talk you out of. But anything the Holy Spirit gives you is yours.

*He who started a good work in you will carry it
on to completion until the day of Christ Jesus.*
Philippians 1:6

One boy said to another, "My daddy has a list
of men that he can whip, and your dad's name
is number one on the list." Little Jimmy went
home and told this to his father.

So Jimmy's daddy went to Billy's daddy and
asked, "Is that right?" Billy's dad said, "Yeah,
that's right." So Jimmy's dad said, "Well, I don't
believe you can do it. What do you think about
that?" Billy's dad answered, "I think I'm going
to take your name off the list."

God never has to take our name off the list. He
never starts anything He can't finish.

*Those He foreknew He also predestined
to be conformed to the image of His Son.*

Romans 8:29

God has a plan for you—you are going to be just like Jesus. He looked at you before you were ever born and saw you receiving Jesus Christ as your personal Lord and Savior. He said, "That one's going to be like Jesus."

Do you know what "predestined" means? Do you see it in the verse above? To be predestined means your destiny is already determined. You are predestined to be like Jesus. So if you are predestined to be like Jesus, there is no question that you will be like Jesus. For what is foreknown in heaven cannot be annulled in hell. It is predestined. It is settled!

Those He called, He also justified;
and those He justified, He also glorified.

Romans 8:30

God already sees you as glorified, brought into your full extent of blessedness in heaven. This is because although you live in history, you actually live above and beyond history. God sees you already glorified in heaven. And if that is true (which it is, of course), then obviously you are predestined to be like the Lord Jesus.

You might say, "I don't feel so glorified right now." Well, He's not finished with you yet. And what He has begun in you, He will complete. You are predestined, and called, and justified, and yes, glorified! You can be absolutely assured of being in heaven with Him.

*By one offering He has perfected forever
those who are sanctified.*
Hebrews 10:14

Notice this little phrase in Hebrews 10:14—
"perfected forever." Jesus hung upon the cross
in agony, never to die again. His one offering
"perfected forever" those of us who are saved.
Not for a little while, not for as long as we live
on the Earth, but for all eternity. His saving of
us will never end.

So what does this biblical fact tell us? Since we
have been saved through the perfect Sacrifice,
we have complete perfection in the Lord Jesus
Christ. When you are saved, God doesn't just
give you a fresh start. He gives you eternal
perfection by that "one offering."

*This man, after offering one sacrifice for sins
forever, sat down at the right hand of God.*
Hebrews 10:12

Nowhere in all the Bible can you find a place
where a person is ever saved twice—any more
than you can find a place where a person was
born physically twice. Just as you were born
physically once, you are born *spiritually* once.

When you were saved, you were marked with a
stamp that said, "Good for one salvation only."
If you were ever to lose that salvation—as if
you could—then Jesus would have to die again
for you to be saved again.

You are saved as many times as Jesus died for
you. Once and only once!

*For the person who knows to do good
and doesn't do it, it is a sin.*

James 4:17

Somebody may say, "Well, what if I sin after I am saved?" We've *all* sinned in the time since we've been saved. Jesus is a Savior, not a probation officer. If I depend on my behavior to keep me saved, then I'll be hopelessly lost.

If you were to follow me around, you might say, "Oh, he doesn't sin." But you'd be sorely mistaken. I don't always do everything I know I ought to do. I wouldn't trust the best fifteen minutes I ever lived to get me into heaven. If we have to depend on our behavior, *I'm* not going to make it, *you're* not going to make it, *no one* is going to make it.

Abraham believed God, and it was
imputed unto him for righteousness.
James 2:23 (KJV)

Do you know what the word "impute" means?
It means to put on one's account. When some-
body has something added to their account in
Bible terms, it's "imputed" to them.

The next time you go to a department store to
buy something, if you want to have a little fun
with the clerk, don't say, "Charge it." Just say,
"Impute it." It means the same thing: "Put that
on my account."

When you were saved, God wrote "righteous"
on your account. You didn't earn it. God put it
on your account apart from your good deeds.

*How happy are those whose lawless acts
are forgiven and whose sins are covered!*

Romans 4:7

We put our faith in Christ, and God calls us righteous. He puts His righteousness into our account. Our statement reads, "How happy are those whose lawless acts are forgiven."

This is something only God can do. If you stole ten dollars from me, for example, then came back and said, "I'm sorry, here's the money I took. Will you forgive me?" I may say, "Sure, I'll forgive you." But I can't cleanse you. I can't remove the fact that you stole the money. All I can do is forgive you. But this Scripture says that our sins are "covered." This means they're blotted out as if they never happened.

*How happy the man whom
the Lord will never charge with sin!*

Romans 4:8

Not only does God impute righteousness, not
only does He forgive, not only does He blot
out our sins, but He promises to "never charge"
us with sin. If God were to put one-half of one
sin on my account, I'd be lost forever. If we
were ever dependent on ourselves for our secu
rity, we would never have it.

You say, "Well, I did pretty good today, but I
did lose my temper in traffic, and I was cross
with my child, and I kicked the cat." Oh, my
friend, your salvation is from God. No, it is not
an excuse to sin, but it is the sweet assurance
that we are eternally free from penalty.

For just as in Adam all die,
so also in Christ all will be made alive.
1 Corinthians 15:22

There are only two representative persons who've ever lived, and we're all part of one of those two—Adam or Christ. In Adam all die; in Christ all are made alive. Everybody is either in Adam or in Christ.

If you're in Christ, that is your new position. What pertains to Jesus pertains to you. And since you are in Christ, the only way you could lose your salvation would be for Christ to lose His relationship with the Father. (Is there any way that could happen?) You are a part of the body of Christ, and it is unthinkable that a part of the body of Christ should perish.

Then the Lord shut him in!
Genesis 7:16

Because God wants us to understand salvation, He gives many illustrations and object lessons in the Bible. Noah's ark is one of those object lessons of salvation.

Why did God shut the door on Noah and his family in the ark? Two reasons: to shut the water out and to shut Noah in. How safe was Noah? As safe as the ark. How safe are we? As safe as Jesus, who is our ark of safety. Noah may have fallen down *inside* the ark, but he never fell *out* of the ark, because God shut him in. God sealed him in, just as we are "sealed with the promised Holy Spirit" (Eph. 1:13).

MARCH 21

If anyone is in Christ, there is a new creation.
2 Corinthians 5:17

A lot of folks believe in eternal security, but here's the kind of eternal security they believe in. They say, "One of these days I'm going to get to heaven and shout, 'Hallelujah, I made it! Here I am in heaven. Thank God I'm secure.' I'll slam the door behind me. I am finally safe in heaven."

Well, what makes you think so? Didn't angels fall from heaven? If you're not secure down here, you won't be secure up there. Security is not found in a place; security is only found in a person. You are eternally secure because of your position in Jesus Christ.

God has given us eternal life,
and this life is in His Son.
1 John 5:11

When do you get eternal life? When you die and go to heaven? No! Sometimes you see a grave marker that reads, "Entered into Eternal Life." No, friend, if you don't have eternal life before you die, you're not going to get it when they put you in the ground. You get eternal life the moment you believe in Jesus Christ.

Jesus said the person who believes in Him "has passed from death to life" (John 5:24). Notice that He says "*has* passed," not "*will* pass." Do you have eternal life right now? If you believe in Jesus Christ, you do. When did you get it? When you believed.

*Everyone who believes in Him
will have eternal life.*
John 3:15

If you have everlasting life, will it ever end? Of course not, because it's everlasting. If it ends, whatever you had wasn't everlasting.

Suppose you were a Christian for ten years, and then you lost your salvation. What did you have? A ten-year life. Suppose you were a Christian for *fifty* years and then lost it? What did you have? A fifty-year life. Whatever it is that you have, if you ever lose it—whatever it was—it wasn't everlasting.

Jesus came to give us present-tense, everlasting life. If you are in Him, you have it right now.

*I am not praying for the world but for those
You have given Me, because they are Yours.*
John 17:9

The passage that is commonly referred to as Jesus' "high priestly" prayer (John 17) is His prayer for the apostles, His original disciples, who were grappling with the announcement of His suffering and death.

And what did He pray? "I am not praying that You take them out of the world but that You protect them from the evil one" (John 17:15). He didn't ask the Father to take them immediately to heaven, but to keep them safe from the enemy as they waited for the full expression of eternal life. This is what He is praying for you, even now, even today.

*I have prayed for you
that your faith may not fail.*
Luke 22:32

Did the Lord Jesus ever pray a prayer that was not answered? Of course not! That's because He always prayed to do the will of the Father. He always prayed in faith. Sin never inhibited His prayer. Every prayer that He prayed was answered.

So just as He prayed for the apostle Peter, whom Jesus said the devil had asked to "sift like wheat" (Luke 22:31), Jesus prays that the Father would keep you. This was the same Peter who cursed and denied Christ yet went on to become the flaming apostle of Pentecost. That's because Jesus prayed for him, just as He prays for you.

I pray not only for these, but also for those who believe in Me through their message.
John 17:20

You may say, "Sure, Peter was prayed for, and James and Matthew and the rest of them. But Jesus never prayed for me like that."

Friend, I ask you to read again the verse from Jesus' high priestly prayer that appears at the top of this page—the same prayer in which He prayed that His disciples would be kept safe eternally in the arms of their heavenly Father. Just write your name down, because He might as well have put your name there. His prayer for your security is a prayer that transcends the centuries with a delayed detonation. Jesus has prayed for you to live with Him forever.

He is also able to save to the uttermost
those who come to God through Him.
Hebrews 7:25 (NKJV)

"To save to the uttermost"—do you know what that means? It means to save all the way, to save you to the end, because (as the verse goes on to say) "He always lives to make intercession" for you, His believing disciple.

The finished work of Jesus is Calvary. He died on the cross and said, "It is finished." But the unfinished work is His ministry of intercession. He continues to pray for us. The One who said, "Father, I thank You that You have heard Me" (John 11:41) is sure to have His prayer for you answered. Your place in heaven with Him is assured if you have placed your faith in Jesus.

An inheritance that is imperishable, uncorrupted,
and unfading, kept in heaven for you.
1 Peter 1:4

I have children and grandchildren, and I want
to tell you this: if someone wanted to harm
them, if somebody wanted to snatch them away
from their family, away from the ones who love
them, I would do anything I could to keep that
from happening. You would too. If you were in
a place of authority, able to put a stop to this
kind of harm and destruction, you would move
heaven and earth to prevent it.

But like me, you're only human. You don't have
all power. God, however, is able to keep safe
those who have been entrusted to His care. He
has the power, and He will do it.

*To those who are the called, loved by God
the Father and kept by Jesus Christ.*
Jude 1

There's a treasure laid up in glory for you. The
lawyers can't get it, inflation can't touch it, the
gnawing tooth of time and the foul breath of
decay can't destroy it. It's there. It's your inheri
tance as a child of God.

People say, "Just pray for me that I'll hold out
faithful to the end." I understand that. It's good
for us to pray for one another that we'll be
faithful Christians. But it's not our holding out;
it's His holding us. We are kept by the power of
God. It's not a matter of our holding on to
Him; its a matter of Him holding onto us,
which He has promised and is faithful to do.

*My Father, who has given
them to Me, is greater than all.*
John 10:29

Can you imagine a power that is strong enough
to pry open the hand of God and take you out
of it? Some people say, "I think the devil could
take you away from God." Oh, you do? You
think the devil can take you away? Well, then,
if he could, why hasn't he?

Think about it. Has the devil been nice to you?
Are you telling me he has the power to remove
you from Christ's hand, but he just hasn't felt
like doing it? No, you're not going to heaven by
the goodness of the devil. You are going by the
grace of God, and the only reason why the devil
hasn't taken you away is because he can't.

*The Spirit's law of life in Christ Jesus has set
you free from the law of sin and of death.*

Romans 8:2

Don't ever get the idea that because you're eternally secure, it makes no difference how you live any more. Some people say, "If I believe in eternal security, I can just get saved and then sin all I want to."

I assure you, I sin all I want to. I actually sin *more* than I want to, because I *don't* want to. Nothing would please me more than knowing I would never sin again. One of these days, when God is finished with me, I'll never sin again. Won't that be wonderful? If you still want to, you need to get your "wanter" fixed. You need to be born again.

April

What Happens When a Christian Sins

*According to Your abundant
compassion, blot out my rebellion.*
Psalm 51:1

If we can't lose our salvation, does that mean we have nothing to lose when we sin?

In Psalm 51, we find King David's reaction to a horrible, heinous, hurtful sin he committed. And yet he was a child of God. I expect to meet David in heaven, don't you? He was a man after God's own heart, and yet . . . he committed the awful sins of adultery and murder.

What we see is this—if a person is bound to sin, he is bound to suffer, as Psalm 51 expresses. He will not lose his salvation, but suffering follows sin as night follows day.

You discipline a man with punishment for sin,
consuming like a moth what is precious to him.

Psalm 39:11

A former prizefighter argued frequently with a certain atheist over the validity of the Bible. One day, the fighter said, "If I can prove to you that just one verse in the Bible is true, will you apologize to me?" The man answered, "Yes." With that the prizefighter reached out and twisted the man's nose so severely that blood ran from both nostrils. Then the fighter opened his Bible and read from Proverbs 30:33: "For the churning of milk produces butter, and twisting a nose draws blood."

And as surely as that is true, so is this: if you sin, you will suffer—whether saved or lost.

Wash away my guilt,
and cleanse me from my sin.
Psalm 51:2

David was a king. He dressed in royal robes. He slept on silken sheets. He bathed in his marble tub with his perfumed soap. Yet his sin made him feel grimy and dirty.

Did you know that if you're a child of God and you sin, you're going to feel dirty spiritually? And if you *don't* feel dirty when you sin, you need to ask yourself if you've ever been saved.

No pig has ever said, "Woe is me, I'm dirty." That's because a pig has no concept of being dirty. Dirt is his element. But the child of God realizes he is dirty when he sins.

If we walk in the light . . . the blood of Jesus
His Son cleanses us from all sin.

1 John 1:7

A lot of people have a form or external practice of religion, but they've never been cleansed to begin with. They've been starched and ironed, but they've never been washed. They have this dirt that's just there all the time, so they never really feel dirty. Dirty is just the way they are.

But when a true child of God sins, he or she feels unclean. If you're a follower of Christ and you've sinned, you've certainly felt that. So I sense the need to repeat myself from yesterday, asking you to give this serious thought: if you can sin and don't feel dirty and grimy, ask yourself, "Do I really know the Lord?"

I am conscious of my rebellion,
and my sin is always before me.
Psalm 51:3

Think about what David was saying in this haunting verse: "My sin is always before me." Day and night, night and day. What David had done was etched so deeply into his conscience and reverberated so loudly through his spirit, he was conscious of it all the time.

Being able to sin is not a test of your salvation. But being able to sin and just ignore it or forget it—that is a danger spot, because God will not let you forget it. The Holy Spirit will put His finger on the sore spot and push, as He did for David. When a believer is living in willful sin, he can't get away from it.

APRIL 6

Godly grief produces a repentance not to be regretted and leading to salvation.
2 Corinthians 7:10

There may be sin in your heart and life, either in your conscious or subconscious mind. You may kick it out the front door, but it will run around the house and come in the basement window. It will show up as an irritable temper, the inability to concentrate, sleepless nights, lack of joy.

There are two kinds of wounds that can come to the human soul. One is guilt, and the other is sorrow. Sorrow is a clean wound. Give it time and it will heal. But guilt is a dirty wound. It just festers and festers and festers and never stops until it is cleansed.

*Against You—You alone—I have sinned
and done this evil in Your sight.*

Psalm 51:4

Against whom did David sin? When you think about it, you might say, "Well, he committed adultery, so he sinned against his own body. He certainly sinned against his wife. And not only did he sin against his body and his wife, he also sinned against his children and family, and even against the entire nation he served as king. His sin of murder, too, was certainly a sinful act against his mistress's husband and her family."

But none of these are mentioned in the verse from Psalm 51 above. David saw his sin for what it actually was—an affront in the face of Almighty God.

You will cry out from an anguished heart,
and you will lament out of a broken spirit.
Isaiah 65:14

When people want to commit adultery, sometimes they go off to some secret rendezvous or hidden place. But it dawned on David, "My God, You were watching me. Your eyes saw what I did. Not only have I broken Your law, but I have broken your heart."

An unsaved man sometimes feels bad about what his sin does to himself, but a saved man feels bad about what his sin does to God. When a slave disobeys, he is only afraid of the whip. But when a son disobeys, he is hurt by his father's displeasure. It's not the punishment but the sin that stings his conscience.

The lips of the righteous feed many,
but fools die for lack of sense.

Proverbs 10:21

The most miserable person on earth is not a lost person but a saved person who is out of fellowship with God. That's because only one thing can take joy from his heart—not two, not three, not four—just one—and yet he has allowed it to happen.

That one thing is *sin*.

If you were to slap me in the face, that could not take the joy out of my heart. It may hurt. It may take away my happiness, but it could not take away my joy. The only thing that has the power to sap joy from a believer is his own sin.

*A good man produces good
out of the good storeroom of his heart.*
Luke 6:45

If you want to see who a person really is, don't watch his actions; watch his *reactions*

It is a person's reactions to life's circumstances and situations that reveal what is truly in his heart. Watch when somebody steals my parking place or cuts me off on the expressway. The way I react is the real me.

If you want to see what a person is full of, see what spills out when he's jostled. If you jostle somebody and anger spills out, they're full of anger. But if you jostle somebody and Jesus spills out, they're full of Jesus.

I have spoken these things to you so that My joy may be in you and your joy may be complete.
John 15:11

You wouldn't want to be happy all the time. To be happy all the time would be like having ice cream for every meal. You'd eventually get sick and tired of it.

Jesus was a man of sorrows. Jesus wept. He was not happy all the time, but he *was* full of joy. Even when He was facing Calvary, He was talking about joy. Paul wrote from a dismal prison, "Rejoice in the Lord always" (Phil. 4:4).

The joy of the Lord is constant. Happiness is like a thermometer; it *registers* conditions. But joy is like a thermostat; it *controls* conditions.

Let me hear joy and gladness;
let the bones You have crushed rejoice.

Psalm 51:8

Remember that this psalm of David is poetry. He didn't really have any compound fractures when he talked about his bones being broken. He was using a figure of speech, just as we do. Even today you might say, "I was just crushed." What do you mean by that?

It doesn't mean that somebody put you into a trash compactor. But it does mean that you are being squeezed in. There's pressure on you. David is saying, "God, you are squeezing the life out of me. I need to feel your joy and gladness again." Without repentance, sin in your life can actually make your body sick.

A joyful heart is good medicine,
but a broken spirit dries up the bones.
Proverbs 17:22

Sometimes we have the idea that if we sin, God is just going to toss us off. Oh no, He doesn't toss us off: He squeezes us all the tighter.

That's one of the ways we know we are saved. God will not let us go. He loves us enough to squeeze us until we drop the sin in our life, the sin that is polluting our body and blocking the free flow of joy.

Take it from this proverb. In the same way that joy works like "good medicine," misery works like a poison, drying us up and leaving us feeling tired, sore, and out of sorts.

A joyful heart makes a face cheerful,
but a sad heart produces a broken spirit.
Proverbs 15:13

A family sits down to dinner, and everything is fine until the son asks, "Dad, can I use the car tonight?" His sister pipes up, "No, you can't use the car tonight. You used it last night. It's my night to use the car." Pretty soon, *they're* shouting, both of the *parents* are shouting, and the whole dinner is ruined because of the uproar. Finally, everybody gets up and leaves in a huff.

Thirty minutes later, one of them calls out across the house, "Has anybody seen the Pepto-Bismol?" You know what has happened. Their bodies have reacted to their hearts. Sin just eats away at us like that—body, soul, and spirit.

This is why many are sick and ill
among you, and many have fallen sleep.
1 Corinthians 11:30

I was reading that a mother who gets into fits of temper can cause the baby who is nursing at her breast to become colicky. That's because we are a unit. We're all tied together.

That's also why Paul could write the verse above to those in the Corinthian church who were acting irreverently at the Lord's table. Their sin was making them ill.

When you're happy in Jesus, you sleep better, you digest your food correctly, your juices flow, your glands secrete as they ought—all because you have joy in the Lord.

Why do you look down on your brother? For we will all stand before the judgment seat of God.
Romans 14:10

If I had my choice for company, I'd rather be around a sinner who has never been saved than a saved person who is out of fellowship with God. Some of the most irritating people you'll ever meet are Christians who are out of joint spiritually. In fact, one way to tell if people are backsliding is to see if they're beginning to develop a critical spirit. Nothing pleases them.

In any church, there are all kinds of things to criticize in people. And when someone is keeping God at arm's length, that person will begin focusing on the faults of those for whom Jesus died. Sin always breeds a sour spirit.

Why do you look at the speck in your brother's eye but don't notice the log in your own eye?
Matthew 7:3

In 2 Samuel 12, Nathan the prophet came to call on David, and subtly confronted him with his sin by telling him the story of a rich man who stole the only lamb of a poor family.

Reading this, you'll be amazed at how quickly David judged this other man. He judged the man for stealing a lamb; David had stolen a woman. He judged him for killing an animal; David had killed a man. He, with the cross tie in his own eye, was going to try to pick a speck out of somebody else's eye. The backslider is always that way; he always has a sour spirit, a vile spirit, finding fault in everybody else.

When you judge another, you condemn yourself,
since you, the judge, do the same things.

Romans 2:1

A man in a small church—one of those people who believe they're God's appointed to make sure everything is done right—opened a door to a closet one day and found five brand new brooms inside. He immediately went to the church treasurer and said, "Why have we spent all this money on five brooms? We're not even meeting our budget. How would you feel if you saw everything you had given to the church tied up in brooms?"

Folks who are out of fellowship with God are quick to find fault with other people. It's one of the trademarks of sin's presence in their lives.

*Save me from the guilt of bloodshed, God . . .
and my tongue will sing of Your righteousness.*
Psalm 51:14

When people don't sing in the song service at church, do you know what the main reason is? They're not filled with the Spirit. They're filled with sin instead. They've lost their song because they've lost their testimony.

Sometimes in church you'll see people who just sit there with their arms folded, who seem to say, "Bless me if you can." Why aren't they able to fellowship with others? What's keeping them from being happy? Why can't they say, "Glory to God"? Why can't they lift their hearts to Jesus in praise? It's because something inside is not right. Sin robs us of our song.

*Because you have forgotten Me and cast Me
behind your back, you must bear the consequences.*
Ezekiel 23:35

Andrew Murray once said there are two classes
of Christians—soulwinners and backsliders.
Manley Beasley used to say, "When you get
right with God, you will have to backslide to
keep from winning souls."

What are the consequences of sin in the life of
a Christian? It dirties the soul, it dominates the
mind, it disgraces the Lord, it depresses the
heart, it diseases the body, it defiles the spirit,
and it destroys the testimony. Can a Christian
sin? Oh yes. But can a Christian sin and not
suffer? No. Being a believer does not exempt us
from paying the consequences of our behavior.

*God proves His own love for us in that while we
were still sinners Christ died for us!*
Romans 5:8

God does not love us because we're valuable;
we are valuable because God loves us. He does
not love us because we are good. We need to
have confidence that no matter what we have
done, God loves us.

Never tell a child who is tempted to do wrong,
"If you do that, God won't love you anymore."
That's a lie. There's nothing you can do to make
Him love you any more—or to make Him love
you any less. Your sin may break His heart, but
He loves you. If we could only understand how
much God loves us, and that for a multitude of
sins, there is a multitude of mercies.

We believe we are saved
through the grace of the Lord Jesus.
Acts 15:11

A family put the following ad in the "Lost and Found" section of the paper: "Lost Dog: Crippled in front paw, blind in left eye, mange on back and neck, tail missing. Recently neutered. Answers to the name 'Lucky.'"

He truly was a lucky dog, because in spite of all that was wrong with him, somebody loved him enough to want him.

Actually, we're all lucky dogs. Even better, we're blessed dogs. God loves us out of sheer grace. Marvel of marvels! Wonder of wonders! God loves us with an everlasting love.

Because of Your name, Lord,
forgive my sin, for it is great.
Psalm 25:11

Notice what David calls his sin in this verse from Psalm 25: "*My* sin."

Yes, it's our sin, not somebody else's. We must be willing to say to God, "I am the sinner. I am the one who has rebelled against you. I must acknowledge my sin, my own transgression, my own disobedience against Your Word."

As the old spiritual says, "It's not my brother, not my sister, but it's me, O Lord, standing in the need of prayer." There's one thing that God will never accept for sin, and that is an alibi. Jesus did not die for alibis; He died for sin.

*If we confess our sins, He is faithful
and righteous to forgive us our sins.*
1 John 1:9

The word "confess" as used in the New Testament is made up of two words: *homos* and *lego*. It means "to say the same thing."

To *admit* your sin is not to *confess* your sin. You may admit your sin in a courtroom, but a confession of sin means to say the same thing God says about it. He says, "This is wrong." And I say, "God, I agree with You. I come over on Your side. I say about that sin what You say about it." No excuses. For as the Scripture says, "The one who conceals his sins will not prosper, but whoever confesses and renounces them will find mercy" (Prov. 28:13).

*Do not call anything impure
that God has made clean.*
Acts 11:9 (NIV)

Learn the difference between satanic accusation and Holy Spirit conviction. The devil is the accuser of the brethren. He will frequently accuse you about sin that has already been confessed.

Yes, he will try to dig it up again. But friend, when God buries it, it is gone. He will never bring you into double jeopardy.

So when the devil accuses you about things you did years ago, remember—you've put it under the blood and have been forgiven, no matter how many times your enemy dredges it up.

When He comes, He will convict the world
about sin, righteousness, and judgment.
John 16:8

The devil will try to make you feel guilty for no reason. You just kind of feel bad all over. It's vague and groundless. That is *accusation*.

But *conviction* is the Holy Spirit saying, like a good doctor as he pushes on a sore spot, "This is where the problem is." He calls it by name because He wants you to confess it so that you can be cleansed.

Don't let the devil accuse you of sin that's been forgiven or of things you've never done. Trust the Holy Spirit to convict you specifically so that you can deal with it and be done with it.

Wash yourselves. Cleanse yourselves.
Remove your evil deeds from My sight.
Isaiah 1:16

If you are aware of conscious, willful sin in your life, you know that it makes you feel dirty and in need of a spiritual bath. Sin is defiling, and it makes you yearn for cleansing.

So reach out for the refreshing power of God's grace. "Though your sins are like scarlet, they will be as white as snow; though they are as red as crimson, they will be like wool" (Isa. 1:18).

You don't have to carry that baggage around any longer. Even if you're guilty of one of those industrial-strength sins like David was, you can be washed. You can be clean.

Purify me with hyssop, and I will be clean;
wash me, and I will be whiter than snow.
Psalm 51:7

A woman had bought an expensive new dress to go out with her husband on their wedding anniversary. But at dinner that night, she spilled some cherry dessert on it. She took it to the cleaners the next day, and when she returned to pick it up, she asked, "Did you get the stain out?" The lady answered, "We did our very best. If you look at it carefully, you may be able to still see the stain. But the average person would never be able to tell it." Yet she never wore it again. She knew the stain was there.

There is no stain that the blood of Jesus can't remove. You can be free from sin's mark.

A little sleep, a little slumber . . .
and your poverty will come like a robber.
Proverbs 6:10–11

Do you know what got David into trouble in the first place? He wasn't doing what he should have been doing. The Bible says it was the time when kings went to war. But the evening found David just getting up from sleep. That rascal had been in bed all afternoon! He got up, looked from his rooftop, and saw Bathsheba.

Did you know that if you're doing what you ought to be doing, you can't be doing what you ought *not* to be doing? An idle mind is the devil's workshop, as the old saying goes. That's the reason why sins of omission are greater than the sins of commission.

Restore the joy of Your salvation to me,
and give me a willing spirit.
Psalm 51:12

God doesn't just cleanse us so that we can sit around and be clean. He puts us back on the track of service. When you sin—once you get your heart clean—get back to work. Apply the four steps of restoration: confidence, confession, cleansing, and consecration.

Don't get the idea that just because you can be cleansed, it makes no difference whether or not you sin. Just as surely as you put your hand on a hot stove and get burned, you're bound to suffer if you sin. But thank God for His wonderful, marvelous, matchless grace that forgives and restores the sinning Christian.

MAY

HOW TO HANDLE
TEMPTATION

*Whoever thinks he stands
must be careful not to fall!*
1 Corinthians 10:12

Temptation is all around. We don't have to go looking for it. We are not tempted because we are sinful. Jesus was tempted. We are tempted because we are human. But if handled rightly, temptations can bring us closer to God.

Unfortunately, however, we live in a generation where many say, "Whatever is natural is beautiful, and whatever is beautiful must be right, so if it feels good, do it." A lot of people live this way, but you know what? That's really on the animal plane. Don't be like the lady who said, "I can overcome anything but temptation." Don't give in to it.

Cursed is the man who trusts in mankind,
who makes human flesh his strength.
Jeremiah 17:5

The only thing worse than giving in to temptation is to fight it in the strength of our flesh, constantly struggling yet constantly failing. It's like the little boy sitting under an apple tree. A man asked, "Are you trying to steal an apple?" The boy answered, "No, I'm trying *not* to."

I heard of a man on a diet who had to drive past a doughnut shop on his way to work. One morning, temptation beckoned to him and he said, "I'll stop only if there's a place to park by the front door." Sure enough, after circling the block three times, he found his parking place! Trying to fight temptation is a sure way to fail.

MAY 3

*God is faithful and He will not allow you
to be tempted beyond what you are able.*

1 Corinthians 10:13

The way to overcome temptation is to over
come through the Lord Jesus Christ. So I want
you to cheer up. *There is help.* Believe it or not,
you can live victoriously over whatever form of
temptaion is bombarding you today, whether
you are being tempted in the area of overeating,
tempted in the area of lust, tempted in the area
of laziness, tempted in the area of greed.

Whatever it is, you don't have to be a slave any
more to the world, the flesh, and the devil. As
the verse above continues, "with the tempta
tion He will also provide a way of escape, so
that you are able to bear it."

Since He Himself was tested and has suffered,
He is able to help those who are tested.
Hebrews 2:18

Don't get the idea that when you get saved, you won't be susceptible to temptation any longer. You *will* be tempted. Being saved does not make you immune to temptation, and being tempted is not a sin.

But the person who is in the greatest danger is the one who is trying to fight temptation in his own strength. He thinks, "I don't need to read a book on temptation. I can overcome it." But without Christ you cannot. God has to make your way of escape for you. His plan is not to remove all temptation from you or to give you immunity, but to give you victory.

You give us victory over our foes.

Psalm 44:7

Football is quite a game. A team takes a bagful of zipped-up air, pointed on each end, and vows to carry it to the other end of the field. The eleven players on the other side of the line say, "No, you're not!" The first team replies, "Oh, yes, we are."

But why do they wait until Sunday afternoon to do it? Why not just go out on a Thursday when the other team isn't there, when they can score on every play? Because there is no glory in that. There's no victory in playing on an empty field. God's plan is for us to have victory, to triumph through the Lord Jesus Christ.

If anyone loves the world,
love for the Father is not in him.
1 John 2:15

The "world" is the enemy out there. I'm not talking about the Earth. God created the world we inhabit; it is not evil. Nor am I talking about the *people* of the world. The Bible says that God loved the world (the world of people) and gave His own Son to redeem them.

When John said, "Do not love the world or the things that belong to the world," he was talking about the world system. The word that is translated as "world" in this verse is the Greek word *cosmos*, meaning "a system, an order of things." The "world" is a way of thinking, living, and relating that is contrary to God's ways.

Your beauty . . . should consist
of the hidden person of the heart.
1 Peter 3:3–4

When Peter wrote in this verse about not putting so much emphasis on our clothes, our hair, and our personal appearance, he wasn't making an injunction against looking nice. He was simply saying that these items are not to be our definition of true beauty.

No, these things are not wrong in themselves: "elaborate hairstyles and the wearing of gold ornaments or fine clothes." But these things can squeeze us into a mold. If we're not careful, we can easily embrace the value system of the world—the external foe—and find ourselves being drawn away from the Lord.

We too all previously lived among them . . .
carrying out the inclinations of our flesh.

Ephesians 2:3

Just as we have an external foe—the world—we also have an internal foe—the flesh. The Bible uses the word "flesh" to refer to our predisposition toward sin, the old Adamic nature that we inherited from our parents, which they also inherited from *their* parents. Like it or not, we all have an enemy inside. You know it's there. It's present in all of us.

Do you ever have to teach a little child to lie? No, you have to teach a child to tell the truth. You don't have to teach a child to be selfish. You have to teach him *not* to be selfish. We all have an enemy inside the gates.

*Each person is tempted when he is drawn away
and enticed by his own evil desires.*

James 1:14

Some like to say, "The devil made me do it."
But if the devil were to evaporate, you'd still go
on sinning. You can't blame everything on the
devil. There's enough inside each of us to sin.

A little boy spit on his sister, hit her with a
broomstick, and called her a bad name. His
mother said to this recalcitrant child, "Johnny,
why did you do that? That is so bad. The devil
must have made you do it." He said, "Well, the
devil made me call her a bad name and hit her
with a broomstick, but spitting on her was my
idea." I think we'd be surprised if we knew how
many of our temptations are really our idea.

Our battle is not against flesh and blood.
Ephesians 6:12

It's true that we have both an external and an internal foe that are working mightily against us, luring us away from our Lord and Savior. But we also have an *infernal* foe. You have an enemy—Lucifer, the devil. He is your foe. He has a plan to sabotage your life and bring death to your happiness. He wants to utterly destroy your purity, health, and wholeness.

Yes, the devil is real and is organized against us. As this verse goes on to say, our fight is against "the rulers, against the authorities, against the world powers of this darkness, against the spiritual forces of evil in the heavens."

*They will come against her
from every side in the day of disaster.*

Jeremiah 51:2

Whatever the temptation, it comes from one of these three sources:

- The world—the external foe
- The flesh—the internal foe
- The devil—the infernal foe

Together they comprise an unholy trinity of temptation that constantly works against us. Think of your flesh as a pool of gasoline. Think of the world as a lighted match. Think of the devil as the one who strikes the match and throws it into the flammable substance. Then you can see how temptation comes about.

*May your spirit, soul, and body
be kept sound and blameless.*
1 Thessalonians 5:23

God is a triune God—Father, Son, and Holy Spirit. And because we have been created in His image, we too have a tri-unity to our own nature, each part of which is highly susceptible to temptation.

The most obvious point of temptation is the *body*, because it and its appetites are the part of us we can see. Another seat of temptation is our *soul*—our mind, emotion, and will—our sense of humor, intellect, and taste. The third is our *spirit*, that part of us that can know, fellowship, and commune with God. Temptation comes to us in each of these areas.

I wholly followed the Lord my God.

Joshua 14:8 (NKJV)

We are made to know three worlds:

• With our physical life, we are able to know the world *beneath* us.
• With our psychological life, we can know the world *around* us and *within* us.
• With our spiritual life, we possess ability to know the world *above* us.

Plants have a body, but they do not have either a soul or spirit. Animals have a body and soul (a conscious life), but they can't commune with God, pray, conceive of eternity, or be redeemed by the love of Christ. Only man has a spirit.

Deliver me from all my transgressions;
do not make me the taunt of fools.

Psalm 39:8

When my body is right, I'm healthy. When my soul is right, I'm happy. When my spirit is right, I'm holy. And that's the way God intended for man to be. That's the way Adam was when he came off the assembly line—healthy in his body, happy in his soul, holy in his spirit.

Most people, however, are unhealthy, unhappy, and unholy. They are out of whack because they're not what God created them to be. That's what sin has done to the human race. The devil has tempted us in body, soul, and spirit. In fact, those are the only places you *can* be tempted, because that's all there is.

Do not be conformed to this age, but be transformed by the renewing of your mind.

Romans 12:2

Remember that you have three enemies—the world, the flesh, and the devil. You're going to find that each of these enemies will attack you in a particular part of your nature—body, soul, or spirit.

The *world's* primary point of attack, for example, is the soul—your ego, mind, emotion, and will. When you break it down into its most basic terms, a worldly Christian is a person whose mind, will, and emotions—all the things that make up his personality and traits, his habits and tastes—have been squeezed into an ungodly mold. The world targets our soul.

Lot chose the entire Jordan Valley for himself.
Genesis 13:11

When a man gets a certain amount of wealth, he doesn't need any more. Even Bill Gates can only eat one meal at a time, wear one suit of clothes at a time, sleep on one bed at a time. When men get beyond that point, they are not making money; they're keeping score.

What Abraham's nephew Lot wanted (in their famous debate over dividing the land) was to be the biggest rancher in all of Canaan. The world was attacking his ego, his soul. He was like many modern Americans. We may have "In God We Trust" on our money, but we have "Me First" on our hearts.

For this is God's will, your sanctification:
that you abstain from sexual immorality.

1 Thessalonians 4:3

Just as the world targets our soul, the flesh takes aim at our bodies. The body is not evil, but the old flesh will tempt us in the area of our body and physical life. We're talking about sins of gluttony, violence, impurity, perversion. The flesh takes our physical body and makes it a vehicle for the expression of sensual sin.

That's why when God says, "Flee fornication" or "You shall not commit adultery," He is not trying to keep us *from* sex; He is trying to keep sex *for* us. The devil is a pervert who will twist everything that is good and righteous and holy. He uses our flesh to work against our body.

Pride comes before destruction,
and an arrogant spirit before a fall.
Proverbs 16:18

Where does the devil war against us? This may surprise you, but the devil comes against us in the area of our spirit. Remember, your spirit is the part of your nature that enables you to know and worship God, and that is the one thing the devil does not want. He wants to drive a wedge between you and God.

The devil doesn't necessarily want you to be a drunk. He'd rather you be a self-confident man of distinction at the country club who thinks he can handle it all. The devil is not against religion and manners. He'd just as soon send you to hell from the pew as from the gutter.

Simon, Simon, look out!
Satan has asked to sift you like wheat.
Luke 22:31

Where was Satan working on Peter when he tempted him to deny Jesus? He tempted him on his faith, on his relationship with God. Peter wasn't on an ego trip. It wasn't his soul that was under attack. It wasn't that his hormones were raging or that he was set on committing some sexual sin. No, his *spirit* was under attack. His faith became weakened under the hammering of Satan's temptation.

Satan will come against you in the same way. And when he does, the Bible tells us to use the "shield of faith" to protect ourselves from "the flaming arrows of the evil one" (Eph. 6:16).

The Devil is prowling around like a roaring lion, looking for anyone he can devour.
1 Peter 5:8

Temptations come through life in waves and seasons. When we're young, for example, most of our temptations are in the realm of the body—sex, drugs, violence, laziness. Through middle age, temptations come mainly from the world against our souls—wanting a greener lawn, a bigger house, a sportier car, a more successful career, more achievements.

But you know what happens when we get old? We've figured out that we're too young to run around like kids. We know we're not the big shot we always wanted to be. So the devil comes after our spirit, tempting us to doubt and fear.

This is the victory that has
conquered the world: our faith.
1 John 5:4

How do you ever gain victory over the wild array of temptations in your life? When you understand how the devil is working, how the flesh is working, and how the world is working, you begin to see the keys to defeating them.

When battling against our external foe—the world—the key word to remember is *faith*. It is faith that overcomes the world. John continues in verse 5: "And who is the one who conquers the world but the one who believes that Jesus is the Son of God?" It is not just faith in a general sense that overcomes the world. Faith that sees Jesus as the Son of God is conquering faith.

*Whoever wants to be the
world's friend becomes God's enemy.*

James 4:4

How do we fight the "world" with our "faith"? Remember that a worldly Christian is someone on an ego trip, somebody trying to satisfy life's hidden hunger with an ungodly system of values. And what is a Christian? It's somebody who has seen Jesus with the eye of faith, who realizes how wonderful He is and has found his or her satisfaction in the Lord.

It's not that becoming "the world's friend" makes you incapable of loving the Father the way you should. In fact, it is just the opposite: you become the world's friend whenever the love of God is not in you.

For I do not trust in my bow,
and my sword does not bring me victory.
Psalm 44:6

You're driving down the road when a little red light comes up on your dashboard, shaped like an oil can. If you know anything about cars, you realize that this light is a warning. It means you're low on oil in your crankcase, and if you continue to drive, you'll burn up the engine.

But what if you took out a hammer from under your seat and broke the light? Would that be a good idea? Of course not! Attacking the warning light is not the answer. You never win by fighting the world, but by filling your spiritual crankcase with Jesus. It is faith that makes Him a victorious reality in our lives.

They scavenge for food;
they growl if they are not satisfied.
Psalm 59:15

What if you were to offer me a wonderful meal—a sizzling steak, a baked potato, a tossed salad, and a tall glass of iced tea? (Oh, and some key lime pie for dessert!) And then, after eating, suppose I go outside, and somebody hands me a plate of stale crumbs and says, "How would you like some of this?" I'd say, "No, thank you, I'm already satisfied." When you're fed on Jesus, you don't have to be in the back alley eating tin cans with the devil's billy goats.

Worldliness only has a pull on those who are hungry for it. A worldly Christian is a person who has not found his satisfaction in Jesus.

*Flee from youthful passions, and pursue
righteousness, faith, love, and peace.*
2 Timothy 2:22

When battling against the internal foe—the
flesh—the key word is *flight*. The sins of the
body, the misuse or corruption of our normal,
human desires for food, sex, comfort, and other
worthwhile pleasures, are not to be overcome
by fighting. We are told to run from them.

Paul taught us that there is a path that leads
away from temptation for those who put their
trust in Christ. "With the temptation He will
also provide a way of escape, so that you are
able to bear it" (1 Cor. 10:13). Sometimes that
way of escape is the King's highway—two legs
and a hard run. Just get out of there.

*Can a man embrace fire
and his clothes not be burned?*

Proverbs 6:27

Jesus taught us to pray this prayer every day: "Lead us not into temptation." Don't watch the garbage on television. Don't read magazines that glorify impurity and appeal to the baser appetites of the flesh. Why put that into your mind? You are flirting with temptation.

You say, "Oh, I can read those dirty magazines and they don't bother me." If you're a man who enjoys browsing through that kind of material, and you say it doesn't bother you, you're either no man, a superman, or a liar. No, you can't put a fire in your bosom and not be burned. You should just flee from those things.

As dry grass shrivels in the flame,
so their roots will become like something rotten.
Isaiah 5:24

If you're wanting to lose weight, make sure to get those Twinkies out of the house. If you're trying to stop smoking, don't keep a cigarette carton in the dresser. You *will* go back to it.

I thank God that I married a virgin and went to the marriage altar as a virgin. But I had plenty of temptations. Every boy does. They told me, "A boy becomes what he thinks about." It's a wonder, then, that I didn't become a girl! In college I kept a motto on my desk: "He who would not fall down ought not to walk in slippery places." Don't see how close you can get. It's like playing with matches and dry grass.

Leaving his garment in her hand,
he escaped and ran outside.
Genesis 39:12

Joseph was the housekeeper and manager for Potiphar, the head of the Egyptian army. But he came under fleshly attack from his master's wife. She wanted to have an affair with him. One day she grabbed him by his clothes and tried to pull him into bed. Joseph was petrified! He came out of his coat and left it in her hand, saturating the place with his absence.

Some people today, rather than getting out of there, would have said, "Let's kneel down by the bed and pray about this." Look, you can't reason with or resist the sins of the flesh. Run as fast as you can in the opposite direction.

Submit to God. But resist the Devil,
and he will flee from you.

James 4:7

When we come to the devil, we are in a battle. The Bible's advice is not to run from him but to stand your ground in the security of your relationship with Christ—and watch as God causes the devil to run from *you!*

So never try running from the devil—never!—because you can't outrun him. Whenever you get where you're going, he'll already be there ahead of you, ready to resume his attack. Instead of running, turn around and resist the devil in the name of the Lord Jesus Christ. Against the world, *faith* against the flesh, *flight;* but against the devil, *fight!*

They conquered him by the blood of the Lamb
and by the word of their testimony.
Revelation 12:11

People say, "I'm not afraid of the devil." But that's not really the big question, is it? The more appropriate question to ask is this: "Is the devil afraid of you?"

He ought to be.

That's because you can come against him in the name of Jesus, and he will flee from you. It's not because you're so strong and fearsome, but you have the power of the resurrected Lord flowing within you through the indwelling presence of the Holy Spirit. With Him as your strength, you can actually overcome the devil.

Resist him, firm in the faith.
1 Peter 5:9

The next time the devil gets on your trail, and you understand he is trying to drive a wedge between you and God, you don't have to take it. You can resist him.

First, make sure any sin in your life has been confessed and repented of. With your heart clean, say to the devil, "I come against you in the name of Jesus Christ. My sin is under His blood. So you have no right or authority to my life. You're trespassing on my Father's property. In the name of Jesus, be gone!" Some may say, "Isn't that like praying to the devil?" I'm not praying to a cat when I say, "Scat!"

JUNE

BELIEVER'S BAPTISM

There is one body and one Spirit . . .
one Lord, one faith, one baptism,
Ephesians 4:4–5

Baptism is one of the most meaningful experiences in the Christian life. You will be greatly blessed if you submit to it. I am not speaking about church tradition but Bible baptism.

You might sometimes hear someone refer to it as "that Baptist doctrine of baptism by immersion." It is not a Baptist doctrine. If Baptists have Baptist doctrine, they need to get rid of it. We also need to do away with Methodist and Episcopalian and Roman Catholic doctrine, and just do what the Bible says. If it is in the Bible, say, "That is God's Word, and that's what I'm going to stand on."

*As many of you as have been baptized
into Christ have put on Christ.*
Galatians 3:27

Someone may say, "Baptism is just incidental. It really doesn't make any difference." It is *not* incidental; it is fundamental. Don't ever mini mize what God has maximized.

Think of the ministry of Jesus, which lasted three and a half years. How did He commence His ministry? By being baptized. How did He then conclude His ministry? By commanding baptism (Matt. 28:18–20).

We are not to minimize something that Jesus taught so strongly and emphasized so much. It is an important part of the Christian life.

In those days Jesus came from Nazareth in Galilee and was baptized in the Jordan by John.

Mark 1:9

Let's see how Jesus Christ was baptized. The river referred to in this verse—the Jordan—is the north-to-south artery that flows from the Sea of Galilee and empties into the Dead Sea. Jesus was not baptized *near* the Jordan or *with* the Jordan but *in* the Jordan.

Verse 10 continues: "As soon as He came up out of the water, He saw the heavens being torn open and the Spirit descending to Him like a dove." Now, if He came up out of the water, where was He? *Down in* the water! Black print on white paper makes it obvious that Jesus was baptized by immersion.

JUNE 4

*John also was baptizing in Aenon near Salim,
because there was plenty of water there.*
John 3:23

Why did Jesus take this trip from Galilee to the Jordan? It was a journey of about sixty miles. So it was obviously not a baptism of convenience. Moreover, John wasn't down there baptizing because of the scenery. I've been there, and it is not a pretty place.

But we don't have to guess why John was baptizing there. The Bible tells us: "There was plenty of water there." If we baptize by sprinkling, we could baptize seven thousand people with a jugful. The reason why John was baptizing in this particular location was because it provided him enough water to baptize by immersion.

*Those who accepted his message were baptized,
and that day about 3,000 people were added.*
Acts 2:41

Sometimes it is inconvenient to baptize. I was
in Kenya once, where we went to visit the tribe
of tall warriors called the Masai. We traveled
miles and miles before finally reaching the little
Masai village where our missionary friend had
been preaching the gospel.

When these tribesmen got saved, they wanted
to be baptized. But there was no pond there, so
they dug a pit and lined it with plastic. Then
they hauled water to it and poured it in. Why
all the difficulty? Wouldn't it have been easier
to take out a canteen and sprinkle everybody?
Not and be obedient to the Scriptures.

Can anyone withhold water
and prevent these from being baptized?
Acts 10:47

In the first church I pastored after I got out of school, the baptistry had a small water pipe with a diameter about the size of my thumb. It took a long time to fill the baptistry.

I announced one day that we were going to have baptismal services on a Sunday afternoon. But when I got to the church, the baptistry was bone dry. I knew there no way to fill it in time. I prayed, "O God, what am I going to do?" In a moment of inspiration, I phoned the fire department and said, "Do you guys specialize in emergencies?" They came and filled it with rusty water, but we got the people baptized!

JUNE 7

Many of the Corinthians, when they heard,
believed and were baptized.

Acts 18:8

The first person I baptized as a young pastor was Willie Vereen, a woman I led to Christ. She wanted to be baptized, but I didn't know how. I hardly knew where to take hold of the person, but that didn't stop us from slithering down a muddy creek bank on a chilly day in Florida. When her feet hit the water, she shivered all over. But we went anyway, and I baptized her.

It's not convenient to baptize this way. But too many people are looking for convenience rather than standing on conviction. Soon I'm expecting churches to start receiving members over the phone and baptizing their photographs!

JUNE 8

The eunuch said, "Look, there's water! What would keep me from being baptized?"
Acts 8:36

Philip met an Ethiopian man who had been to Jerusalem to worship and was traveling home. Philip went up to the man's chariot and led him to Christ. The man wanted to be baptized.

Now, this man served as treasurer for Queen Candace of Ethiopia. He was traveling by chariot. You know they had drinking water. You know they had bathing water. When the man said, "Look, there's water!" it wasn't that they needed a little cupful for a sprinkling service.

Bible baptism is by immersion. It is not always convenient, but this is the method of baptism.

*Get up and be baptized, and wash away
your sins by calling on His name.*
Acts 22:16

Baptism by immersion was originally practiced
by all branches of the early church. Baptism by
sprinkling or pouring initially began as a way
to baptize the sick or bedridden, but immersion was always the preferred method.

This is evident in the writings of the early
church fathers. Tertullian, writing in AD 200.
Cyril, bishop of Jerusalem, AD 348. The early
second-century Epistle of Barnabas describes
Christian baptism as immersion. Hippolytus
preserves an early baptismal creed in his writings. The Roman Catholic church did not
adopt sprinkling until the thirteenth century.

*On hearing this, they were baptized
in the name of the Lord Jesus.*

Acts 19:5

Many of the founders and leaders of denomi
nations that practice sprinkling today have in
their writings acknowledged immersion as the
original biblical method.

George Whitefield (Methodist). Conybeare
and Howson (Episcopalian). John Calvin (Pres
byterian). Martin Luther (Lutheran). Philip
Schaff (Lutheran). As a matter of fact, if you
travel to Europe and go into some of the old
cathedrals—Roman Catholic churches built
before the thirteenth century—you'll find that
a number of them have baptistries in them
much like the ones in churches that immerse.

*They were baptized by him in the
Jordan River as they confessed their sins.*

Matthew 3:6

Did you know the word "baptize" is basically an untranslated word in your Bible? It's really a Greek word, meaning "to immerse."

In 1611, when King James of England commissioned scholars to translate the Scriptures into English, they went back to the original Greek manuscripts. But when they came to this word, it created a problem. The word was used in ordinary language, not as a religious word. A woman doing dishes would *baptize* her dishes. It's just a plain, run-of-the-mill, everyday word, not necessarily a religious word. But it now has great religious significance: "to immerse."

As he proclaimed the good news . . .
both men and women were baptized.
Acts 8:12

The word "baptize" has been transliterated—taken from one language and put into another. Why didn't they translate it?

The King James scholars had a problem. If they translated that word as "sprinkling," anybody who knew Greek would have laughed them out of the kingdom. But if they translated it as "immerse," it would have been a source of embarrassment to the king, whose church practiced sprinkling. So what you read in your Bible is an untranslated word. They just took the word *baptizo*, made a new English word out of it, and placed it into the English language.

JUNE 13

All of us who were baptized into Christ Jesus were baptized into His death.

Romans 6:3

When reading the word "baptize," you can just do your own translation in your mind. The word means "to immerse." Other Greek words mean "to pour" or "to sprinkle," but Scripture doesn't use any other words for baptism. It only uses the word *baptizo*.

People say, "Ah, but sprinkling is taught in the Bible." They'll find a ceremony somewhere that talks about the sprinkling of water or blood. Granted, the word "sprinkling" is used, but it has nothing to do with baptism. I defy anyone to show me anywhere in the Bible where sprinkling is taught as a form of baptism.

*We have been joined with Him
in the likeness of His death.*

Romans 6:5

This passage says that baptism is a picture of the death, burial, and resurrection of Jesus Christ—and of our death, burial, and resurrection with Him. Remember, baptism pictures and symbolizes the saving gospel of Christ. That's the reason why we must adhere to the method, because if you change the method, you destroy the picture.

Baptism is a living, repeating portrait of the gospel. It pictures our identification with the Lord. "For in that He died, He died to sin once for all; but in that He lives, He lives to God" (Rom. 6:10). This is baptism's testimony.

*Christ died for our sins . . . He was
buried . . . He was raised on the third day.*
1 Corinthians 15:3–4

Suppose you've never seen my wife, Joyce, and
you say, "Adrian, are you married?" I would say,
"Yes." Then you might ask, "What is your wife
like? Do you have a picture of her?" I'd say,
"Yes, I do. Would you like to see it?"

I would reach into my billfold and pull out a
picture. What if, though, I pulled out a picture
of a race car or a waterfall or a coffee table.
You'd say, "That's your *wife?*" I would say, "No,
but any old picture will do." Wouldn't that be
ridiculous? If it doesn't look like her, why
should I give you another picture? Baptism can
only be a picture of the reality it represents.

We were buried with Him by baptism . . .
so we too may walk in a new way of life.
Romans 6:4

When I got baptized, it was a funeral for the old Adrian. Baptism pictured the burial. The only mourner in attendance was the devil, who hated to see me die, because I was his good buddy when the old Adrian was still alive.

So here's the reason why someone should never be baptized before he or she is saved. It would be like having your funeral and being buried before you die.

When you're saved, you die to the old way. You proclaim, "Good-bye, world, good-bye," and become a new person. Baptism pictures that!

*Right away he and all
his family were baptized.*
Acts 16:33

The great ingathering of souls recorded on the Day of Pentecost in Acts 2 affirms that a person must first receive the word of the gospel, and then be baptized. Those of Cornelius's house in Acts 10 followed the same procedure: they first received the Holy Spirit, and then they were baptized.

In Acts 16, Paul and Silas said to the Philippian jailer, "Believe on the Lord Jesus, and you will be saved" (v. 31). That same hour of the night, he and his family were baptized. First he heard the word of the Lord, believed on Jesus, and then was baptized. This is the biblical order.

*Having been buried with Him in baptism,
you were also raised with Him through faith.*

Colossians 2:12

When you're baptized, you're picturing your death with Jesus. But baptism not only pictures the *burial* of Jesus—and your burial with Him—it also pictures the resurrection of Jesus and your resurrection with Him. Not only are you buried by baptism, but you are raised again, according to the Scripture.

See, it's more than submersion; it's *immersion* What's the difference? With submersion, you may not come back up. But with immersion, you go down *into* the water only to come back up *out* of the water. We bid farewell to the old world; we say hello to the new man.

Sown in dishonor, raised in glory;
sown in weakness, raised in power.
1 Corinthians 15:43

Just think of what baptism pictures. I have been delivered from my sin! My sin is buried in the grave of God's forgetfulness—hallelujah! I am a new person.

Baptism not only pictures my death with Him as well as my resurrection life with Him, but it also pictures my ultimate glorification with Him. One of these days, I am going to have a body like the resurrected body of the Lord Jesus Christ. All of this is pictured in baptism—the death, burial, and resurrection of Jesus for our sin, and our identification with His death, burial, and resurrection.

*We have died to what held us, so that we may
serve in the new way of the Spirit.*

Romans 7:6

If you were the devil, and you could take any
message out of the church—but only one!—
which one would you want to take out? You
wouldn't even have to think about it. The devil
doesn't care what you believe as long as you
don't believe the gospel.

And what is the one ordinance of the church
that teaches the gospel over and over and over
again? It is baptism.

The devil has done a slick job on some people,
some pastors, and some churches to take away
this wonderful picture of the gospel.

*If we died with Christ, we believe
that we will also live with Him.*

Romans 6:8

Suppose I were to die, and you somehow—and for some reason—were able to haul me out of the graveyard and say, "Let's bury Adrian." If you put a few grains of sand on my head and left me to bake in the sun, that would be a disgrace. You can't bury me with a few grains of sand, any more than you can bury me in a few drops of water.

We were buried with Him by baptism into His death. What does baptism symbolize? It pictures Calvary. It pictures Easter. It pictures Pentecost. It pictures the Second Coming. All of this is only possible by the practice of immersion.

I am not ashamed of the gospel,
because it is God's power for salvation.

Romans 1:16

You are identified with the Lord Jesus when you are baptized. Baptism shows that you are a new man or woman, and that you have a new master. It shows that you are not ashamed of Christ. When you are baptized in front of all those people, you are saying to each of them, "I believe in Jesus."

In the Bible, the confession of faith was not walking down the church aisle. Many times they didn't have church buildings at all. So the confession of faith was baptism. When one got baptized, he or she was saying, "I believe in Jesus Christ, and I am not ashamed of Him."

Christ did not send me to baptize,
but to preach the gospel.
1 Corinthians 1:17

Don't ever believe that baptism saves you or even helps to save you. It is a picture of what happened to you when you *were* saved.

It's like the wedding ring I wear. That ring does not make me married. I could still be married and not wear it. But that ring means I'm not ashamed of Joyce, that I'm not trying to fool anybody. My ring is a symbol that I am a married man and that I belong to her.

Once you have been saved, you should be baptized whenever possible, as soon as possible. But never, ever mistake its symbolism.

*I am not ashamed, because
I know whom I have believed.*

2 Timothy 1:12

One Sunday morning during children's church, a little boy prayed to receive the Lord Jesus into his heart. The children's minister said to him, "Go tell the pastor that you have been saved and that you need to be baptized."

So the little boy did as he was told and went to the pastor to relay the message: "Look, I have been saved. I need to get advertised."

I like that! Because that is what baptism is. When you get baptized, you're getting advertised. You're saying to the watching world, "Hey, look! I belong to Jesus Christ."

Then fear fell on all of them, and the name
of the Lord Jesus was magnified.
Acts 19:17

I have seen it happen so many times: when a person gets baptized, his friends and loved ones fall under conviction. Baptism is preaching the gospel of Jesus Christ without saying a word. It's a silent but graphic sermon.

Who would not want to preach that sermon before his loved ones? Who would not want to give that testimony if he was truly saved? I am convinced that some women don't want to get baptized because they don't want to mess up their $25.00 hairdo. But there is a Master to confess and a message to convey about the One who hung naked on a cross in agony for you.

*Go, therefore, and make disciples
of all nations, baptizing them.*
Matthew 28:19

Jesus did not request you to be baptized; He commanded you to be baptized.

Now suppose I were to have a coronary and fall down on the ground, trying to say something. You would say, "Listen to him. He's dying. These are his last words."

When Jesus was concluding His ministry, He had some last words before He went back to heaven, including a command about baptizing disciples "in the name of the Father and of the Son and of the Holy Spirit, teaching them to observe everything I have commanded you."

For whoever has, to him more will be given.
Mark 4:25 (NKJV)

While baptism is not necessary to salvation, it is necessary to obedience. And obedience is necessary to joy and fruitfulness in the Christian life.

You may wonder, "Why can't I understand more of the Bible?" Well, the way to understand the parts of the Bible you *don't* understand is to obey the parts you *do* understand. If you know that God has instructed you to be baptized but you haven't yet obeyed Him, why should He teach you anything else? When you begin to obey, you'll be surprised how much more light will break into your life.

I call to God, and the Lord will save me.
Psalm 55:16

Before we move out of this month and on to another topic, I want to make clear that baptism either with a spoonful or a tank full cannot take away sin. You can be saved anytime, any place, anywhere.

If baptism is necessary to salvation, than a man in the desert couldn't be saved. A man in an airplane couldn't be saved. A man in a submarine—though surrounded by the depths of the ocean—couldn't be saved because there's not enough water inside his vessel to be baptized in. No, anytime anyone calls upon Jesus in repentance and faith, that person is saved.

These are a shadow of what was to come;
the substance is the Messiah.

Colossians 2:17

During the time when Lyndon Johnson was president, a friend of mine and his family were visiting the Smithsonian Museum of American History in Washington, D.C. While standing in the "First Ladies' Collection" exhibit, which featured wax figures of our nation's first ladies in their inaugural gowns, they noticed a woman standing beside them. It really *was* Lady Bird Johnson, who had come to see the exhibit.

Just then, a man with a camera asked her if she would step aside so he could get a picture of Lady Bird's wax statue. Never substitute the symbol of baptism for the reality of salvation.

We were all baptized by one Spirit into one body—whether Jews or Greeks . . . slaves or free.
1 Corinthians 12:13

Let's sum up our look at believer's baptism as taught in the Bible. Baptism has a method, a meaning, and a motive.

• *The method*—immersion. Remember, if you change the method, you destroy the meaning.
• *The meaning*—a picture of our identification with the death, burial, and resurrection of Jesus, which is the gospel.
• *The motive*—to confess Christ, to obey Him, and to declare His saving gospel.

If you are saved and not baptized, make plans to participate in this wonderful experience.

July

How to Discern
the Will of God

*You led them with a pillar of cloud by day,
and with a pillar of fire by night.*
Nehemiah 9:12

There are about six myths concerning the will of God, and I want to help destroy them all. The first is the "Map Myth"—that God is going to give you a road map that spells out every detail of His will for you.

The will of God is not a road map; it is a relationship. He doesn't say, "Five years from now, you're going to be doing this or that, and then ten years from now, you'll be over here for two or three months." Like the children of Israel, who followed Him by the presence of cloud by day and fire by night, just know that He is leading you by His continual presence.

I delight to do Your will, my God;
Your instruction resides within me.
Psalm 40:8

The second myth to deal with is the "Misery Myth"—if I do the will of God, it's going to be painful. Those who buy into this misconception believe that God is some cosmic killjoy. They think if they tell Him that they will do anything He wants them to do, He will send them as a missionary to deepest Africa to be eaten by cannibals.

Some people are afraid of God and are equally as afraid to surrender to Him. Yet God is a loving God who wants for us what we would want for ourselves . . . if only we had enough sense to want it.

I, the Lord, the God of Israel
call you by your name.
Isaiah 45:3

The "Missionary Myth" implies that God's will is only reserved for a certain class of people, that God calls preachers and missionaries but He doesn't call ordinary people.

But just as God has a plan for the evangelist, He has a plan for the secretary. He not only has a plan for the preacher, He has a plan for the plumber. He has a plan for the banker as well as the Bible teacher. He has a plan for all of us.

Never think, "Only missionaries and preachers can sense God's call on their lives." Report for duty whoever you are.

After the fire there was a voice, a soft whisper.
1 Kings 19:12

Another misunderstanding about God's will is the "Miracle Myth"—implying that you must have something dramatic happen in order for you to obtain His guidance and direction.

Many people want to be "earthquakers" when it comes to discerning God's will. They want a cyclone, a forest fire, an inferno. But if you want to find out generally the will of God for your life, there's a still, small voice. There's a path "like the light of dawn, shining brighter and brighter until midday" (Prov. 4:18). First it's dark, then it's gray dawn, then you see colors and shadows, then high noon.

I will repay you for the years
that the swarming locust ate.
Joel 2:25

Perhaps you have fallen prey to the "Missed-It Myth." You say, "When I was young, God had a plan for my life, but I missed it. I think maybe He wanted me to be a missionary, but now that I'm old, it's too late for me."

My friend, it is never too late for you when it comes to being part of God's kingdom plan on Earth. He has a will and purpose for you at every stage of your life. You may have missed God's original plan, but that doesn't mean you are without hope for being used by Him ever again. If you've had some years that you think were wasted, let God give you a fresh start.

JULY 6

Lord, restore us to Yourself, so we may return;
renew our days as in former times.
Lamentations 5:21

Every guided missile has a plan, a trajectory, a carefully prescribed path for it to fly. Yet hardly a one of them ever flies according to its original plan. They have on-board computers that cause the thrusters to yaw and gimbal, correcting and adjusting, replanning its intended path. But it's never out of control.

If you believe you have missed God's plan, let Him reprogram you where you are. Think how awful it would be, for example, if one of those missiles turned around and headed back to the launching pad. Don't rebel against God, but don't think it's too late for you to do His will.

*I also will love him
and will reveal Myself to him.*

John 14:21

Lastly, there's the "Mystery Myth"—that God's will is a mystery, sort of like an Easter egg hunt. God says, "There's something I want you to do, but I'm not going to tell you what it is. You search around and see if you can find it."

It would be like saying to my son, "I have some things I want you to do that will make you very happy. But if you don't do them, I'm going to punish you, and you'll be unhappy." He would say, "Well, what do you want me to do?" And I would say, "I'm not going to tell you, but you'd better do it." That's kind of absurd, isn't it? God *wants* you to know His will!

So he, trembling and astonished, said,
"Lord, what do You want me to do?"
Acts 9:6 (NKJV)

If you met Jesus face-to-face and could ask Him one question, what would it be? I think I know what I would ask: "Lord, what do You want me to do?"

The apostle Paul asked Him that question on the road to Damascus in Acts 9. Actually, he asked Jesus two questions: first, "Who are You, Lord?" and second, "What do You want me to do?" Can you think of two greater questions?

Paul spent the remainder of his life learning the answers—who Jesus is, and what Jesus wanted him to do. We need to ask the same questions.

JULY 9

*It is not in man who walks
to direct his own steps.*
Jeremiah 10:23 (NKJV)

Ours is an age when we're no longer surprised by anything. Modern technology is growing and expanding and coming at us so fast, it is like we are drinking from a fire hose.

Yet man could rightly be described as a clever creature who has lost his way in the dark. Even in this age of instant information, our world is filled with misguided men and women. People *want* to know God's will for their lives, but we simply cannot know it in and of ourselves.

We just don't have what it takes to discern the will of God. It is He who must reveal it to us.

For we are His creation—
created in Christ Jesus for good works.
Ephesians 2:10

This verse teaches that we are God's workman ship. We have not only been saved by His grace but have been created "for good works, which God prepared ahead of time so that we should walk in them."

Yes, God has a plan ordained for us . . . before it ever comes to pass. Isn't that wonderful?

David, writing under the inspiration of the Holy Spirit, declared, "A man's steps are estab lished by the Lord, and He takes pleasure in his way" (Ps. 37:23). It is not up to us to figure all this out. It is ours to live what He shows us.

I will instruct you and show you the way to go;
with My eye on you, I will give counsel.
Psalm 32:8

When my children were little, I would some
times see them misbehaving in the second or
third pew. No one else would know it, but from
my vantage point at the pulpit, I could look at
them—even while I was preaching—and say
with my eye: "If you don't straighten up, you
are going to be punished when we get home."

Men, have you ever been in a restaurant, you
start a line of conversation, and your wife looks
at you as if to say, "Don't go there"? We should
have this kind of intimate relationship with the
Lord, as well—where He can guide us with His
eye, instructing us in the way we should go.

Many plans are in a man's heart,
but the Lord's decree will prevail.
Proverbs 19:21

God has a great, overarching, sovereign will—a
prevailing will. And He can never ultimately be
thwarted in these purposes.

He also has a *permissive* will, by granting man a
free will that we may use to disobey Him.

In addition, He has a *personal* will for each one
of us. He has as many plans as He has people.
He has a plan for your life and mine.

It is our great desire to know His will, a great
delight to do it, and a great danger to refuse it.
Nothing is right for you if it is not God's will.

*Even the hairs of your head
have all been counted.*
Matthew 10:30

It is God's *prevailing will* that the kingdoms of this world will become the kingdoms of our Lord and of His Christ. That will happen.

It is God's *permissive will* that we make right choices, obeying His Word.

It was God's *personal will* for me that I marry Joyce. He brought her to me.

God has a plan for each one of us, amazing as this is to conceive. It is like the president being interested in a piece of driftwood in the ocean for God to be interested in us, but He is!

*You are not willing to come to Me
that you may have life.*

John 5:40

Sometimes, when people want to build a house, they already have in mind the kind of place they want. Maybe they've drawn it on paper at the kitchen table. So by the time they consult an architect, they're not really asking him to design their house from scratch. They're saying, "This is what we want; we just want you to go design it."

I'm afraid we come to God like that sometimes. We say, "Lord, here's what I want for my life. Now, go design a plan for me." We're asking Him to conform His will to ours. But we will never know God's will if we don't want it.

Then they will call me, but I won't answer;
they will search for me, but won't find me.

Proverbs 1:28

I heard about a vagabond who spent his entire life walking across the country. Someone asked him, "How do you decide where you're going?" He said, "It really doesn't matter. I just go." They asked, "But what if you come to a fork in the road? Which way do you do go then?" He said, "I pick up a stick, throw it in the air, and whichever way it lands, that's the way I go." Then he added, "Sometimes I have to throw it six or seven times to get it to land right."

A lot of us are like that. We say we want to know God's will, but we keep on throwing the stick until it lands the way we want it to go.

He leads the humble in what is right
and teaches them His way.

Psalm 25:9

In the old days, when cowboys would take a wild stallion and break him, they called that "making him meek." They didn't cripple him. No, they wanted him to keep his strength; they wanted him to still have his fire and speed. But they also wanted to be able to put a saddle and bridle on the stallion.

Is God able to put a saddle and bridle on you? Have you ever come to the place where you say, "Do whatever You want with me"? Or have you been like a teenager who drops out of school, who says, "They can't teach me anything"? If that's your attitude, you're probably right.

Samuel responded,
"Speak, for Your servant is listening."
1 Samuel 3:10

Do you have a quiet time? If God speaks with a quiet voice, you need to have a quiet time and place to hear it. If you're around a lot of furor and hubbub and noise, and somebody is whispering, you're not going to hear it. That's the reason why you need to have a quiet time, so that you can pray, "Lord, what is it You really want me to do?"

Our prayer needs to be listening as well as talking. Have you had a conversation with someone who does all the talking? Sometimes our prayer is, "Listen, Lord, Your servant is speaking," not "Speak, Lord, Your servant is listening."

The Lord said to him in a vision, "Ananias!"
"Here I am, Lord!" he said.

Acts 9:10

It is not enough to *know* the will of God. You have to *yield* to the will of God. It's not enough to *hear* God. You have to say, "Lord, I am ready to do Your will."

In the account of Saul's conversion in Acts 9, we learn that God sent a messenger to instruct him. This man, Ananias, found out from God that Saul was a chosen vessel to spread the gospel of Jesus Christ to the world. To read this story is to see a once-proud Pharisee—Saul of Tarsus—yielding to instructions from a little known disciple of Jesus. That is what yieldness looks like in a person's life.

Shouldn't we submit even more
to the Father of spirits and live?
Hebrews 12:9

Imagine a man coming into a service station with an old automobile. All four tires are flat, the fenders are banged in, there's no water in the radiator, no oil in the crankcase, the gas tank is rusted through. He pushes it right up to the pump and tells the attendant, "Fill 'er up." He answers, "What for?"

If we are not yielded and yet say, "God, show me Your will," He asks, "What for?" If we're not ready to do His will, why should He show it to us? Would you be willing—would you be yielded enough—to sign the contract at the bottom and say, "Now, God, you fill it in"?

*As he traveled and was nearing Damascus, a
light from heaven suddenly flashed around him.*
Acts 9:3

God sometimes directs by miracles. This is not
His ordinary way, but He does at various times
work supernaturally in visions, in dreams, and
in miracles.

He directed Saul of Tarsus by a miracle, when
Jesus appeared to him in a brilliant light on the
road to Damascus. Saul was knocked down
from the force of the experience, and the Lord
spoke to him in an audible voice.

God has never appeared to me that way, but it
is certainly possible. It may not be His norma
tive way, but we dare not discount miracles.

JULY 21

The words of the Lord are pure words,
like silver refined in an earthen furnace.

Psalm 12:6

Saul was already full of the Word of God even before Jesus met him face-to-face, because he had heard Stephen preach one of the greatest sermons ever delivered, just before Stephen was stoned to death. Saul was also a Pharisee, which meant he was steeped in the Word of God. All of this began to come together as the Lord Jesus began speaking to him.

Much of the will of God for your life is found in your Bible. It is foolish—in fact, wicked—to try to discern the will of God apart from the Word of God. If He has said it in His Word, that is His will for you!

Remember your leaders
who have spoken God's word to you.
Hebrews 13:7

You're going to find that God will use other people to help you know His will for your life, just as God used Ananias to help Saul know His will.

Could it be that God is using me right now to help you navigate your way through a cloudy stretch of road in your life? In the same way, you may be used of God to help other people who are caught in confusion and crisis.

You are often going to discover that you find the will of God in the context of a Christian church and with other believers in Christ.

You should wage war with sound guidance—
victory comes with many counselors.
Proverbs 24:6

If you are getting instruction, encouragement, or guidance from a brother or sister, make sure they're walking in the Spirit. God confirmed to Saul that this man who was coming, Ananias, was of Him. And God will confirm the same thing to you.

Thank God for people who give us wise counsel when we're facing difficult decisions and trying to discern His will. God is certainly the final Counselor in all things, and we have to obey Him rather than man. But never become so arrogant that you don't think you can learn from other people.

When the Spirit of truth comes,
He will guide you into all the truth.

John 16:13

Another way that you can know and discern the will of God is through the Spirit of God. His Holy Spirit does lead us when we learn to recognize His voice and to be led by what He reveals to us in our spirits.

"All those led by God's Spirit are God's sons," Paul wrote in Romans 8:14. That's fairly plain and to the point, isn't it? "Led by God's Spirit." Galatians 5:18 says, "If you are led by the Spirit, you are not under the law."

The Holy Spirit of God leads. It is one of His many functions in the life of a believer.

*The Holy Spirit . . . will teach you all things
and remind you of everything I have told you.*
John 14:26

The Holy Spirit never shoves. He guides and
leads. If you feel a hand between your shoulder
blades, just pushing on you, that's most likely
not the Holy Spirit. The Holy Spirit is gentle.

I've met many people who are compulsive and
driven. They're not *led* people. They're generally religious zealots, and usually they're quite
dangerous.

We, however, need to be *led* by the Holy Spirit.
Remember the still, small voice. Yes, it's some-
what of a mystical thing, but it is the living
God communicating His will to you.

*He led His people out like sheep and
guided them like a flock in the wilderness.*

Psalm 78:52

I was in the kitchen one morning when I began to sense, as I was praying, that I should take Joyce to breakfast. And though I don't usually pray about where to eat, I felt impressed to go to a particular restaurant at I-240 and Poplar. So we went. And as we sat there, a man came up to us and said, "I can't believe this! You are the one man in the world I need to see today." He told of some trouble in his home, and said, "My wife would trust you. Would you please talk to her today?" Later, this couple came to our house, and both received Christ into their hearts. Maybe if we all were walking in the Spirit, more things like that would happen.

*Don't be foolish, but understand
what the Lord's will is.*
Ephesians 5:17

Acts 9:20 says that "immediately" after Saul's conversion, "he began proclaiming Jesus in the synagogues." Remember, this was a man who just days earlier had been a vocal, violent hater of Christianity. And right away he's a preacher! "All who heard him were astounded" at the wisdom he proclaimed (Acts 9:21).

God gives wisdom. What is wisdom? It is the ability to see life from God's point of view. When you get saved and are surrendered to Him—when you are walking in the Spirit, filled with the Spirit—you're going to find out that you have the mind of Christ.

If any of you lacks wisdom, he should ask God,
who gives to all generously.

James 1:5

When trying to discern the will of God, don't be afraid to use your mind. Why would God renew your mind if He didn't want you to use it? We have the mind of Christ.

The will of God is not found in getting wet around the lashes and warm around the heart, in getting goose bumps and liver shivers. No, the will of God is sanctified common sense. So get your motives clear, get your heart right, then do what you think is best. As J. I. Packer said, "Wisdom is the power to see and the inclination to choose the best and highest goal, together with the surest means of attaining it."

After many days had passed,
the Jews conspired to kill him.
Acts 9:23

In Acts 9, beginning in verse 23, you find out that when Saul began preaching Jesus, he ran into a lot of difficulty. Jesus didn't come to get us out of trouble; He came to get into trouble with us. It doesn't mean we're out of the will of God when trouble comes. Don't get the idea that it's going to be all honey and no bees.

Just imagine, here was the great Saul—with the equivalent of three Ph.Ds—now a wanted man, a price upon his head, being lowered over the city wall by night to escape a murder plot. Yet he was certainly in the will of God. The Lord's unseen hand guides the affairs of men.

*The one who has seen Me
has seen the Father.*
John 14:9

This is going to sound simplistic when I say it, but take all the principles for discerning the will of God, and you can sum them all up in one word: Jesus. This is not just pious talk. The will of God for you is *Jesus!*

Take all these things—the providence of God, the people of God, the Spirit of God—then put one big, overarching name over it, and it's just Jesus. He may use a lot of different ways to show you His will for your life, but if you concentrate on falling in love with Jesus, the rest will take care of itself. He is Lord, the head of the church. Just surrender to Him.

The world with its lust is passing away,
but the one who does God's will remains forever.
1 John 2:17

Finally, let me give you three principles about the will of God:

1) The will of God is for your welfare. It is not something you *have* to do; it is something you *get* to do.

2) The will of God will never take you where the power of God and the grace of God cannot enable and keep you.

3) God will not force His will on you. You are free to choose. But you are not free to choose the consequences of your choice.

AUGUST

Faith and How
to Have It

*Through Him, we have obtained access by faith
into this grace in which we stand.*

Romans 5:2

Imagine two letters dropped at the post office
to be delivered. One of the letters is on crisp,
expensive stationery. It is beautifully typed and
elegant in language. The other letter is on cheap
paper, written in pencil, smudged, and filled
with bad grammar and misspellings. But it has
one thing the other letter doesn't—a stamp.

Which letter will get delivered?

It is not the eloquence and form of our prayers
that gets them delivered but the stamp of faith.
Like they say, "Pray, believe, and you'll receive.
Pray and doubt; you'll do without."

He touched their eyes, saying,
"Let it be done for you according to your faith!"
Matthew 9:29

I don't know what you will accomplish in your Christian life, but I can tell you the measurement that will define what you do accomplish. It will not be according to your fame. Not according to your feelings. Not according to your fortune. Not according to your friends. Not according to your fate. It will be according to your faith.

If there were ever a time for us to have an earth shaking, mountain-moving, devil-defying faith in Almighty God, this is the time, this is the day, and this is the hour. Faith is the medium of exchange in the kingdom of heaven.

They were broken off by unbelief,
but you stand by faith.
Romans 11:20

When you go to the grocery store, you use dollars to pay for your purchases. But when it comes to the Christian life, you receive from God by faith. As I said before, faith is heaven's medium of exchange. It is by far the greatest asset we have.

Unbelief, on the other hand, is our greatest stumbling block in life. Unbelief is the chief wickedness. Unbelief is the mother sin, the father sin, the parent sin. It is the sin of all sins. Unbelief caused Eve to sin against God in the Garden of Eden. She failed to believe the Word of God.

*So we see that they were
unable to enter because of unbelief.*

Hebrews 3:19

Unbelief is what locked the doors of the Promised Land to the children of Israel. For all the grumbling, bad attitudes, and discontentment that characterized their demeanor after leaving Egypt, it was their unbelief that kept them at a distance from God's promised reward.

Jesus, too, allowed the people's unbelief to tie His hands on His ministry visit to His home town. The Bible clearly says, "He did not do many miracles there because of their unbelief" (Matt. 13:58). The sovereign God has limited Himself to work according to the faith and belief of the people of God.

*Anyone who does not believe
is already condemned.*
John 3:18

What sends people to hell today? It is not lying, not murder, not rape, not arson. It is not sexual perversion, not pride, not arrogance. It is this: unbelief! You see, Jesus *died* for all those other sins. Those sins have been paid for with His blood. It is unbelief—and unbelief alone—that shuts the door to heaven.

In the spiritual realm, *nothing* is possible if you do not believe, but "everything is possible to the one who believes" (Mark 9:23). Just as you live physically by breathing, you live spiritually by faith. As the Bible says, "The righteous will live by faith" (Rom. 1:17).

> *By faith in His name,*
> *His name has made this man strong.*
>
> Acts 3:16

Think of all that comes to us by faith:

- *Salvation*—"Since we have been declared righteous by faith, we have peace with God through our Lord Jesus Christ" (Rom. 5:1).
- *The Holy Spirit*—We receive "the promise of the Spirit through faith" (Gal. 3:14).
- *Victory*—"This is the victory that has conquered the world: our faith" (1 John 5:4).
- *Victory over Satan*—"Take the shield of faith, and with it you will be able to extinguish the flaming arrows of the evil one" (Eph. 6:16).
- *Sanctification*—Jesus told us that we were made holy "by faith" in Him (Acts 26:18).

Return, you faithless children.
I will heal your unfaithfulness.
Jeremiah 3:22

Think of all the problems that come to us when we fail to exercise faith:

- *Worry*—"I don't think I can handle this."
- *Loneliness*—God seems far away.
- *Disobedience*—Violating His Word.
- *Guilt*—Our guilt gland becomes overactive when we don't trust God for cleansing. Faith is our acceptance of God's acceptance of us.

Oh, the blessings of God we receive when we learn to believe in Him. But, oh, the trouble we cause ourselves when we choose not to believe. May He write the difference on our hearts.

Jesus replied to them, "Have faith in God."
Mark 11:22

Faith must have the right object before it can be real faith. Sometimes people say, "Just have faith. Only believe." Whenever a person says to me, "Just have faith," the first question in my mind is, "Faith in what?" They say, "Only believe." I ask, "Only believe what?"

There is no power in faith alone. Don't think there's something mystical or magical about just believing. Your faith is no better than its object. Misplaced faith is dangerous.

It is not *faith* that moves mountains; it is *God* who moves mountains.

No one who believes on Him
will be put to shame.
Romans 10:11

Many people think that faith is the same thing as positive thinking. But faith is a whole lot more than that.

Certainly, it will help you to think positively. There's nothing the least bit wrong with having an upbeat, optimistic perspective on things. In fact, it is healthy to do so. But there is no *power* inherent in positive thinking. It doesn't come with built-in authority and strength.

The reality of biblical faith in Romans 10:11 is that we are to believe on *Him*. Your faith is no better than its object.

*If you do not stand firm in your faith,
then you will not stand at all.*

Isaiah 7:9

If you make faith out to be positive thinking, you're going to get discouraged, because times will come when you'll *try* to think positively but you will not be *able* to think positively.

A little boy came to his dad and said, "Dad, I think I flunked my math test today." His dad said, "That's negative thinking. You've got to be positive, son." To which the little boy replied, "Okay, I'm *positive* I flunked it."

If you look into yourself, trying to think positively, it's going to dawn on you after a while that you don't have what it takes.

Open their eyes that they may turn from darkness to light and from the power of Satan to God.
Acts 26:18

If you put your faith in faith, you're a sitting duck for the devil. He will come to you and say, "You're not good enough to be saved." You say, "I know it, but I don't have faith in myself."

The devil then says, "There are hypocrites in the church." And you say, "I'm not putting my faith in hypocrites, I'm trusting the Lord."

The devil will say to you, "But you don't feel like you should." And you say, "I'm not trusting my feelings. I'm trusting the Lord." As long as your faith is securely in Jesus, the devil can say what he wants, but he cannot defeat you.

This is His command: that we believe in the
name of His Son Jesus Christ.
1 John 3:23

You'd think after a while, the devil would grow
tired and leave us alone when we persist in
declaring that our faith is not in ourselves, in
others, or in our feelings. But then he'll say the
slyest thing of all: "You say you're trusting the
Lord, but how do you know that your faith is
strong enough, that it's the real thing?"

If the devil ever pulls this stunt on you, just tell
him, "Look, devil, I am not putting my faith in
faith; my faith is in Jesus." There's a difference
in that. The least amount of faith in the right
object is always better than strong faith in the
wrong object. We are to believe in Jesus.

Keeping our eyes on Jesus,
the source and perfecter of our faith.
Hebrews 12:2

The Bible tells us that we are to "run with endurance the race that lies before us, keeping our eyes on Jesus"—not looking to ourselves, not putting faith in our faith, but placing the full weight of our trust on God.

The reality of faith is not positive thinking. It's not faith in faith. It is faith in God.

Weak faith in the right object is better than misplaced faith in the wrong object. You ask, "Does God honor weak faith in a person?" He certainly does. If He didn't, most of us would never receive anything from Him.

Immediately the father of the boy cried out,
"I do believe! Help my unbelief."
Mark 9:24

In Mark 9, we read the account of a man who had a little demon-possessed boy. This father came to Jesus and said to him, "If You can do anything, have compassion on us and help us." Jesus answered with a rhetorical question, "'If You can?' Everything is possible to the one who believes" (Mark 9:22–23). That's when the man uttered the words at the top of this page.

Jesus gave this father just what he needed. He had a weak faith, but it was a weak faith in the all-powerful, living God. I'm not saying that we ought to have weak faith, but we must be convinced of the overcoming power of Jesus.

Jesus said to her, "Didn't I tell you that if you believed you would see the glory of God?"
John 11:40

Jesus said to His disciples that the least amount of faith is greater than the greatest amount of difficulty. He said to them, "If you have faith the size of a mustard seed, you will tell this mountain, 'Move from here to there,' and it will move. Nothing will be impossible for you" (Matt. 17:20).

If you want your faith to be strong, do not put your faith in the size, amount, or strength of your own faith. Put your faith in God. That's the way to grow a strong, living, vibrant, and enduring faith. As you find out more and more who God is, your faith will know no bounds.

The life I now live in the flesh,
I live by faith in the Son of God.

Galatians 2:20

If you want to cross a bridge and you don't know whether it will hold you up, you might be afraid and tremble and try to make yourself believe. You might screw up your own courage and hope you have what it takes to cross it. But what if that bridge before you was made of concrete and steel, with semitrucks going over it every day? When you see that kind of bridge and understand what it can sustain, it's easy for you to cross it.

When you see who God is, rather than putting your faith in positive feelings, you just put your faith in God, and your faith will grow.

The people who know their God
will be strong and take action.
Daniel 11:32

During a long, bitterly cold winter, a man tried crossing the frozen Mississippi River on foot. He was confident he could do it; the ice looked crusty and thick enough. But part of the way across, his confidence faltered. He dropped to all fours, trying not to put too much weight on any one place. Soon, his fears rising, he began squirming across the ice on his belly. Just then, he heard a roaring noise, as if the ice was cracking. The roaring grew closer until he finally saw what it was—a man driving a team of horses, hauling a wagonload of cut logs up the river. One man knew only the "strength" of his faith; the second man knew the strength of the ice.

Faith comes from what is heard, and what is heard comes through the message about Christ.

Romans 10:17

All true biblical faith is rooted not only in knowing God but in hearing from the God that you know. As Paul said, "How can they call on Him in whom they have not believed?" (Rom. 10:14).

In order to have faith, you must first hear from God. You cannot know the will of God by guessing at it. The verse above says that faith "comes." You don't generate it. *It comes.* God gives it. "For it has been given to you on Christ's behalf not only to believe in Him, but also to suffer for Him" (Phil. 1:29). Belief is something that is granted to us—given to us—by God.

*Did you receive the Spirit by the works
of the law or by hearing with faith?*
Galatians 3:2

No one can believe God unless God enables him to believe. And how does God enable you to believe? He gives you a word. As the verse said that we referenced yesterday, "Faith comes by hearing, and hearing by the word of God" (Rom. 10:17 NKJV).

Therefore, contrary to the popular belief of some in the Christian community, you don't just "name it and claim it." Rather, you listen for God to speak, then you "believe it and receive it." Faith is not an achievement we earn for ourselves; it's an endowment that is given to us by God.

*We wait for the blessed hope and the appearing
of the glory of our great God and Savior.*

Titus 2:13

What does *hope* mean? To most people today, it
means "maybe." Perhaps a strong desire. But
the word "hope" in the Bible does not mean
the same thing as it does to our modern world.
"Hope" in the biblical sense means a bedrock
assurance based on the promises of God.

That's the reason why the Bible calls the second
coming of Jesus the "blessed hope." This kind
of hope is assurance mingled with anticipation.
It is not a "blessed maybe" but a "blessed assur
ance." How do we know? Because He said so.
He's not here yet, but we know He's coming.
Our hope has an unshakable promise.

Faith is the substance of things hoped for,
the evidence of things not seen.
Hebrews 11:1 *(NKJV)*

You know. of course, what the word "substance" means. Actually, the Greek word translated as "substance" in Hebrews 11:1 is much like our English word. It implies something that is underneath you, something you can stand on.

When you're living by faith, you're not walking around on eggshells and Jello. Friend, faith is not Jello. Why? Because it is the "substance" of things that we hope for, things that God has said and promised in His Word.

The root of faith is the Word of God. You can know it's a sure, substantial place to stand.

The word that you hear is not Mine
but is from the Father who sent Me.

John 14:24

We have been seeing that you cannot have faith unless God speaks. Well, how does God speak? There are two words for "word" in the Greek language. One is *logos,* which we could say is the Bible, the written Word that tells us the living Word. Then there's *rhema,* which means an utterance, a spoken word. We might call it a word from the Word.

As you read the Bible—or the *logos*—the Spirit begins to speak to you out of the Word of God. You get a *rhema* from the *logos.* You receive an utterance from God. He speaks to you, and you hear Him in your heart.

I pray that the God of our Lord Jesus Christ . . .
would give you a spirit of wisdom and revelation.
Ephesians 1:17

The preacher is the mailman who delivers the message, but it is God who gives the message. It is not the sermon outline or the preaching style. It is not the words on the page nor the ink forming the letters. It is the revelation of God, given in Christ, that communicates truth into a believer's heart.

The New American Standard's translation of Romans 10:14 says, "How will they believe whom they have not heard?" Not "*of* whom," just "whom." You must hear God, not merely *from* God. In order to receive and act on faith, you must first get a *rhema* from God.

God spoke to the fathers by the prophets at different times and in different ways.
Hebrews 1:1

How does God speak? It usually happens like this: You're reading the Bible, or you're praying—you're actively opening your spirit to receive what God desires to reveal—and He faithfully puts that portion of truth into your heart. He says, "This is from Me. Everything I speak is true, of course, but this is something especially from Me to you."

You say, "God never speaks to me that way." Well, are you listening for Him? Do you carve out quiet times to be with Him? Are you ready to do His will if He reveals it? Do you want to hear Him? Are you reporting for duty?

The words I speak to you I do not speak on My own. The Father who lives in Me does His works.
John 14:10

What is the result, the purpose of faith? What does biblical faith actually do or accomplish? Faith is not getting man's will done in heaven; it is getting God's will done on earth. The result of faith is the will of God.

Remember that I said you cannot have faith unless you hear from God. Do you know what you're going to hear when you hear from God? You are going to hear the will of God.

When God speaks, He is going to say, "This is what I want done, and therefore, I want you to believe it."

You will be a good servant of Christ Jesus,
nourished by the words of the faith.
1 Timothy 4:6

You cannot have faith for anything that is not the will of God. If it's not His will, why should He supply you with the confidence and trust to pursue it? What would be the point?

Some people think that if they believe hard enough and have faith that God will do something for them or through them, it will come to pass. But the faith that God gives—the only kind of faith that really matters—is designed for the accomplishment and fulfillment of His will, not for our own desires and ends. We don't need genuine faith until we're serious about seeking the will of God.

You are the ones who justify yourselves in the
sight of others, but God knows your hearts.
Luke 16:15

If I had enough faith, could I turn my car into solid gold? Not unless God *wanted* it turned into solid gold. That keeps God in control, see. And that's a good thing.

Remember King Midas? He wished that whatever he touched would turn to gold so he could be wealthy beyond measure. But when he went to eat his food, it turned to gold. When he kissed his beautiful daughter, she was no longer a daughter he could love. What he thought would be a blessing became a curse. We need to be confident in the awareness that God knows this and protects us from ourselves.

*Whenever we ask anything
according to His will, He hears us.*
1 John 5:14

If you could say, "I can believe and have what ever I want," you'd make a mess of things. It would put *you* rather than God in the driver's seat. The result of faith is always that the will of God is done.

You say, "Oh, that means fewer blessings for me." No, it means *more* blessings for you! The will of God is not something you *must* do; it is something you *get* to do.

- The *reality* of faith is faith in God.
- The *root* of faith is in hearing God.
- The *result* of faith is that God's will is done.

*Show me your faith without works,
and I will show you faith from my works.*
James 2:18

How do you release faith? How does faith get down to where it becomes your own personal experience?

True faith does more than just merely believe; *it obeys.* If what you say you believe does not translate itself into action, then you don't really believe it.

The word "believe" in our language comes from the Old English "by live." What we believe, we live by. The rest is just religious talk. So let me tell you what faith is: faith is belief with legs on it. How are you going to release faith today?

*But all did not obey the gospel. For Isaiah says,
"Lord, who has believed our message?"*

Romans 10:16

You may say, "If I can't believe, then it's not my
fault. It's God's fault because He didn't give me
faith. You said no one can believe unless God
speaks to him—and maybe God didn't speak to
me, so it's not my fault."

Oh, God is speaking, but not everybody will
obey. Not everyone will release his or her faith.
God stretches out His hand, but some people
are disobedient and contrary. They parade His
Word past the judgment bar of their mind.
"But isn't faith a gift from God?" they say. Yes.
So is breathing. God gives air and God gives
lungs, but you can smother if you wish.

The goal of our instruction is love from a pure heart, a good conscience, and a sincere faith.
1 Timothy 1:5

Let me sum up with some clear, practical advice on having a victorious faith:

• Be *saturated* with the Scriptures. Remember that faith comes by hearing from God.

• Be *dedicated* to the Savior. It's not so much a great faith in God as it is faith in a great God.

• Be *separated* from sin. Unconfessed sin is a faith killer. If it's not working, try repentance.

• Be *activated* by the Spirit. Remember, faith is belief with legs on it. Get started today!

SEPTEMBER

HOW TO BE FILLED
WITH THE HOLY SPIRIT

*"No," they told him, "we haven't
even heard that there is a Holy Spirit."*
Acts 19:2

Imagine that a man had bought a new car. He invites his friends over to see the flawless paint job, to sit in the soft seats. But everywhere he goes, he has to push it, which can be extremely exhausting. So rather than being a good thing, his car is really more of a burden. But then one day, someone introduces him to the ignition. He discovers that if you put the car in "drive," it can surge forth in power. "Why didn't somebody tell me about this before?" he asks.

"Nobody could be that dumb," you say—unless that person is a Christian who does not understand the power of the Holy Spirit of God.

As for me, I am filled with power
by the Spirit of the Lord.
Micah 3:8

Many Christians don't understand that when they got saved, God implanted an engine into their salvation. I don't mean any disrespect by calling the Holy Spirit an engine, but He is the dynamism, the power of our Christian life.

Some people are like the man and his car. Rather than salvation carrying them, they're the ones always pushing it, grinding out their Christian experience because they haven't yet discovered the wonderful Spirit-filled life. The Spirit will turn your drudgery into dynamism. Rather than making Christianity a burden, He will make it an empowering blessing to you.

Don't get drunk with wine, which leads to
reckless actions, but be filled with the Spirit.
Ephesians 5:18

Suppose your pastor staggered into the pulpit one Sunday morning—thick-tongued, bleary-eyed, his hair disheveled, his clothes rumpled and wrinkled. Someone would say, "I think the pastor is sick." Then someone else who was closer in proximity to him would say, "No, he's drunk!" Tongues would wag. Meetings would be called.

But the same Bible—the same verse—that says not to "get drunk with wine" also says to "be filled with the Spirit." It would be a greater sin for the pastor to show up not filled with the Spirit than to show up drunk.

It would have been better for them not to have known . . . than, after knowing it, to turn back.
2 Peter 2:21

You may not agree with my statement that it would be better for someone to be drunk than to not be filled with the Spirit. But the Bible says it is a greater sin to fail to do what you ought to do, than to do what you ought not. And because you can only do one thing at a time, if you do what you ought to do, you can't be doing what you ought not to do.

By the way, I believe far more harm is done in our churches by people who are not Spirit-filled than by people who are drunks. Far more harm is done by people who are trying to do the work of God in their own flesh.

*The disciples were filled
with joy and the Holy Spirit.*
Acts 13:52

Let's have a little language lesson. When the Bible says, "Be filled," this is in the imperative mood. That means it is necessary, a command, an imperative. "Be filled" is also in the present tense. The question is not, "*Were* you filled?" but "*Are* you filled?" And one more thing: it is plural in number. It literally says, to everyone who is a child of God, "Be *being* filled."

In addition, the biblical command to "be filled" is passive in voice. That means we are acted upon when we are filled by the Spirit. It is not something we can earn or attain. It is a gift from God, who fills us.

Always having everything you need,
you may excel in every good work.
2 Corinthians 9:8

The first reason for being filled with the Holy Spirit is obedience. As we talked about yesterday, being filled with the Spirit is not a good idea, not a suggestion. It is an imperative if we are to be obedient to the Lord.

The second reason for being filled is because of your obligations, to help you accomplish the tasks that are before you. Many people think, "If I just knew what I was supposed to do, then I'd have it made." No, just knowing what to do is not enough. You also need the power to do what you know you ought to do. You can't do it alone. You need the Spirit's empowerment.

*True worshipers will worship
the Father in spirit and truth.*
John 4:23

Have you ever been in a boring worship service?
No, you haven't. Perhaps you have been in a
boring *church* service, but not a boring *worship*
service. Real worship is never boring; rather, it
is invigorating!

But a service that is conducted apart from the
Holy Spirit of God—oh, how "tedious and
tasteless the hours," as the old hymn goes. We
can wear the varnish off the bench trying to get
out of a dry-as-dust church service. How sad to
see a "filled church of empty people trying to
overflow." To keep worship from being routine,
we need to be filled with the Spirit.

*Wives, submit to your own
husbands as to the Lord.*

Ephesians 5:22

In our day of militant feminism, this verse is politically incorrect. Some say, "This makes the wife inferior to the husband." No, it doesn't. Everybody knows that a woman is infinitely superior to a man at being a woman. Submission is an equal party voluntarily placing himself or herself under another equal so that God may be glorified. It has nothing to do with inferiority or superiority. Even God the Son is said to be in submission to God the Father, not because of inferiority but out of authority.

How does a woman learn the spirit of submission? By being filled with the Spirit of God.

*Husbands, love your wives, just as also Christ
loved the church and gave Himself for her.*
Ephesians 5:25

Just as the Bible instructs women to submit to
their husbands, it gives a specific command to
the men as well. But how can a husband love
his wife as Christ loved the church? Only when
he's filled with the Holy Spirit.

Which one is the more difficult task—the wife's
duty to submit, or the husband's duty to love?
I'd say the more difficult task has been assigned
to the husband. He is to love his wife the same
way Christ loved the church. Jesus *died* for the
church! Now that is love. Truly, we need the
Spirit of God within us if we are to be successful in our wedded life.

*Walk in love, as the Messiah also loved us
and gave Himself for us.*
Ephesians 5:2

This is the way Jesus loves the church—the way men are supposed to love their wives:
• sacrificially
• supplyingly
• steadfastly
• selflessly

Most women don't mind being in submission to a man who loves her enough to die for her and who shows it by the way he lives. But in his own strength, a man doesn't have what it takes to do *anything* the way Jesus does. I can't love my wife as Jesus loves me, but Jesus in *me* can love her when I'm filled with His Holy Spirit.

*Slaves, obey your human masters
with fear and trembling . . . as to Christ.*
Ephesians 6:5

When you go to work in the morning, you are to serve your boss as if he were Jesus. You say, "That two-legged devil? I'm supposed to serve him as if he were Jesus?" Read it in your Bible. Isn't that what it says?

My, that just cuts across our grain. Many would say, "I don't give a hoot about my boss. I'll serve Jesus, but I'm not serving *him!*" Oh, to the contrary, you are to serve Jesus *by* serving him. This may, in fact, be your greatest testimony. When the Spirit is filling you full with Himself, your job becomes a lampstand to let your light shine. It becomes your temple of devotion.

*All who are under the yoke as slaves must regard
their own masters to be worthy of all respect.*

1 Timothy 6:1

Do you know what an employer ought to say when he calls the employment agency? "I need some helpers, and by the way, if you have any Christians down there, send them over first. They get here on time, they don't steal, they don't gossip, they work with industry, and I do believe they must think I'm God."

If Christians would begin to live like that on Monday, would others begin believing what is taught on Sunday? No, it is not human nature to live that way. But if you want to be obedient to God like this in your work life, allow yourself to be filled with His Spirit.

The One who is in you is greater
than the one who is in the world.
1 John 4:4

You're in a battle—a spiritual battle. You're not
wrestling with flesh and blood. Your enemy is
not the IRS, not your mother-in-law, not the
Democrats, not the Republicans, not your nosy
neighbor, not your boss. No, the devil is your
enemy. He is the one you're up against.

Therefore, yours is a spiritual battle. And unless
you're filled with the Holy Spirit, you're going
to lose it. See, the devil laughs at our schemes,
he mocks at our organizations, he ridicules our
good intentions—but he fears the Spirit of God
in a holy Christian. In your war life, you need
to be filled with the Holy Spirit.

Pray also for me, that the message may be given to me when I open my mouth.
Ephesians 6:19

Paul was an intellectual, a world traveler, a man who possessed a great mind, and yet he knew like every other preacher—as the hymn lyric so clearly states it—"All is vain unless the Spirit of the Holy One comes down."

That's the reason why the apostles said, "We are witnesses of these things, and so is the Holy Spirit whom God has given to those who obey Him" (Acts 5:32). When I'm preaching, I want the Holy Spirit to say, "That's right! You listen to him, He's telling you the truth." We can be witnesses, but the Holy Spirit is the true witness within those who obey Him.

You can do nothing without Me.
John 15:5

These are evil days, and they are crying out for Spirit-filled people. The world has tried everything, and nothing has worked. Now they're looking to the church, saying, "Is this real?"

But if we are not filled with the Spirit, every opportunity that presents itself and every day that we live is wasted, because we can do "nothing" without Him in our lives. Do you know what "nothing" is? It's a zero with the edges trimmed off. We've got to stop thinking of the Spirit-filled life as being a tonic to remove our own personal stress. No, it is the power to meet the challenges of a world in desperate need.

Walk in wisdom toward outsiders,
making the most of the time.
Colossians 4:5

I heard of a lady who was giving a testimonial about the importance of knowing first aid. She said, "The other day in front of my house, an old man lost control of his car and hit an oak tree head-on. He was thrown out into the street. He had compound fractures in his limbs and was bleeding all over. But just then, I remembered my first aid instruction. I recalled that if I would put my head between my knees, I wouldn't faint."

That's the kind of Christianity a lot of people desire. But we are here as our Lord's representatives—to serve Him wherever we are.

This Spirit He poured out on us abundantly through Jesus Christ our Savior.

Titus 3:6

How can you be filled with the Spirit? It is not your responsibility to persuade God to fill you with His Spirit. Many people think, "If I could just persuade God to fill me with His Spirit, I could finally walk in victory." No, it is not your job to talk Him into it; it is your job to *permit* Him to do it.

God *wants* to fill you with His Spirit. It is His desire to do so. He longs for you to live in the power, freedom, and victory that He alone can provide you. If you have trusted him for salvation through Jesus Christ, His Spirit already lives within you. Now let Him have all of you.

*The Spirit is the One who testifies,
because the Spirit is the truth.*

1 John 5:6

One of the requirements for being filled with
the Holy Spirit is that we bow to Him in full
surrender. Notice that I said "Him." Don't get
the idea that the Holy Spirit is an influence or
quality of some kind. He is a living being.

This doesn't mean He has a body; it means He
has personality. And when I say "personality,"
that doesn't mean He is simply charming to be
around (although He is). It means He thinks.
He wills. He acts. He loves. He is not an "it."
You wouldn't say of me, "It wears a blue blazer."
To be filled with the Holy Spirit is to be filled
with His life, the Spirit of the living God.

*Do you not know that your body is a sanctuary
of the Holy Spirit who is in you?*
1 Corinthians 6:19

Some people misunderstand what we mean by being filled with the Spirit. It is not as if you are some sort of vessel that the Holy Spirit is being poured into, or that He is pouring some "thing" into you, like love or power.

No, you are a temple, and He is a Person. Think of Him as a living entity, a living being—yes, a Person, though of course, much more than a person. He is the Spirit of God—alive, aware, animated, and animating. Think of the Spirit as a Person who wants to come and take control of your body—His temple—to transform you for His holy, glorious purposes.

We are completely open before God.
2 Corinthians 5:11

Suppose a guest came to visit you, and you told him that he was welcome to make himself at home in your house. You really meant that. But the next day when you got home from work, you found him sitting at your desk, going through your bank statements, reading your old love letters, flipping through your personal diary, and making notes about your will. You would say, "Hey, what do you think you're doing?" And he would say, "I thought you told me that I could do anything I wanted here?"

When we tell the Holy Spirit to feel at home in our lives, I wonder if we really mean it?

Everything exposed by the light is made clear.
Ephesians 5:13

Is there any area of your life that is out of bounds to the Holy Spirit? Your financial life? Your sexual life? Your personal life? Your career ambitions? Your recreational hobbies?

Anything? Anywhere?

To be filled with the Spirit means that there is a Person who is completely occupying the temple, the sanctuary of your life—every room, every desk drawer, the key to every closet. Everything now belongs to Him. That's what it means—a complete commitment. You just turn the keys over to Him. Are you ready to do that?

The nations drank her wine;
therefore, the nations go mad.
Jeremiah 51:7

When Paul said, "Don't get drunk with wine…
but be filled with the Spirit" (Eph. 5:18), why
didn't he say, "Don't steal, but be filled" or
"Don't tell lies, but be filled"?

First, he was talking in *contrast.* Being drunk is
the devil's substitute for being filled with the
Spirit. But he was also speaking in *comparison.*
When a person is drunk, he is under the control
of another influence. Therefore, his speech, his
thought patterns, his walk, his perspectives—
everything is changed. Paul was saying that the
Spirit should have that kind of control over us,
changing the way we think, act, and live.

Teach me to do Your will, for You are my God.
May Your gracious Spirit lead me on level ground.
Psalm 143:10

How does a man get drunk? By drinking, right? But how does he stay drunk? He has to keep on drinking. Likewise, it's not enough to be filled with the Holy Spirit one day in the past. You have to *keep* being filled with the Spirit.

It's not something where you say, "Well, that's done. What's next?" No, there are far too many Christians who were once Spirit-filled but now are "sobered up." When it comes to the Spirit of God, we are to continue being filled on an ongoing basis. It begins with complete commitment where you say, "Lord, come take all of my life." It results in His continual control.

*Acknowledge that the Lord is God.
He made us, and we are His!*

Psalm 100:3

Being filled with the Holy Spirit is an exercise of complete commitment, continual control, and a conscious claiming. Yes, you must *claim* the Spirit of God.

How did you get saved? You claimed Christ as your Savior. You are filled the same way. It's not a matter of feeling; it's a matter of filling. You say by faith, "Lord, take control of my life."

Once you have made a complete commitment and surrendered every key of your life to Him, you then have every right to claim heaven's throne gift.

If anyone is thirsty,
he should come to Me and drink!
John 7:37

Suppose you were in the desert, dying of thirst, when someone offered you a tall glass of cool water and said, "Here, drink." Imagine if you said in return, "Yes, water is wonderful. That's just what I need. I am so thirsty." But then you refused to drink it.

For whatever reason, many Christians fail to appropriate what our Lord has offered. They want to be filled with the Spirit, but apparently they don't want to do the things that being filled entails. Remember that God desires to fill you with His Spirit and has promised to do so. Claim His promise by faith . . . and be filled.

*Speaking to one another in psalms, hymns,
and spiritual songs . . . giving thanks always.*
Ephesians 5:19–20

We've looked at the reasons and requirements
for being Spirit-filled. Let's wrap up the month
by looking at the *results* of Spirit-filled living.
Immediately after Paul admonished us not to
"get drunk with wine . . . but be filled with the
Spirit" (Eph. 5:18), he mentioned several things
that should follow as a result: "speaking to one
another . . . singing and making music . . .
giving thanks . . . submitting to one another."

In other words, this will have an effect on:
• our relationship with God
• our relationship with circumstances
• our relationship with other people

*I will sing praises
with the whole of my being.*
Psalm 108:1

Do you know how you can tell if you're Spirit-filled? You'll just be saying all day long, "Jesus, I love You. Jesus, I praise You." When you get in the car, you'll want to sing songs to Him, you'll want to be praising Him, you'll want to lift your hands in worship. You'll find the love of God just pouring out of you.

I tease about not being able to sing, but when I get in the car, I roll up the windows and just sing my heart out to Jesus. I don't let anybody else hear, but I know He'd just as soon hear my singing as someone with a good voice—because He knows He put that song in my heart.

Give thanks in everything,
for this is God's will for you in Christ Jesus.
1 Thessalonians 5:18

A Spirit-filled Christian is not grumbly hateful; he's humbly grateful. He is giving thanks—not sometimes, but always—for all things.

I assure you, friend, there is no way that you can do that apart from being filled with the Holy Spirit. It's the only way. With the Spirit in control, you can be grateful in any situation.

Now, when you praise God even in evil circum stances, it doesn't mean that you approve of the evil. It just means that your trust is in God. It means that no matter what happens, you know that God is greater.

*In humility consider others
as more important than yourselves.*
Philippians 2:3

A Spirit-filled Christian is someone who has learned to accommodate himself to others. He submits to other people. Submission is not for women; it is for Christians.

You hear people say, "I know my rights!" But what rights does a dead person have? We have been crucified with Christ.

I don't submit to you because of you; I submit to you because of Jesus. You submit to me the same way. How wonderful to be around Spirit-filled brothers and sisters who have learned the spirit of accommodation.

They were all filled with the Holy Spirit and
began to speak God's message with boldness.
Acts 4:31

May I ask you a very personal question as we
wrap up this month's devotions? (I'm going to
ask it anyway, so you may as well say yes.)

Are you filled with the Spirit? Right now? No
doubt about it?

This is not simply a request. It is a command
from God to obey. When you are filled with
the Holy Spirit, you'll discover that the automobile you call "salvation" has an engine in it,
and that the ignition key is faith to believe the
Word of God. So hop in—and get ready for
Him to take you for the ride of your life!

OCTOBER

HOW TO DISCOVER
YOUR SPIRITUAL GIFT

OCTOBER 1

Every generous act and
every perfect gift is from above.
James 1:17

Alexander the Great, the conquering general, once gave a beautiful and priceless golden cup to a lowly servant. When the servant saw the gift, he said, "Oh, no, that's too much for me to receive." Alexander drew himself up and said, "It's not too much for me to give."

If I placed a special gift for Joyce on the table, and she didn't even bother to unwrap it—just left it sitting there—two things would happen. I would be really disappointed, and she would not have the joy of receiving what I had given her. You, too, have been given a gift from God. Are you going to unwrap it? Or not?

One and the same Spirit is active in all these,
distributing to each one as He wills.
1 Corinthians 12:11

In the Christian world and way of thinking,
we've often divided people up into the *clergy*—
those who are in full-time ministry—and the
laity—those who are in the pew. A little girl
was asked to describe the difference between
the two. She said, "The clergy are paid for being
good; the laity are good for nothing."

You may not realize it, but if you're saved, you
have been called into the ministry. Yes, God has
a ministry for each and every one of us. Even
your secular job can be your temple of devo
tion and your lampstand of witness. You are a
gifted child, no matter who you are.

*Be diligent to present yourself approved to God,
a worker who doesn't need to be ashamed.*

2 Timothy 2:15

There are three kinds of people in nearly every church—those who make things happen, those who watch things happen, and those who don't even know that anything *is* happening. Most, unfortunately, are the watchers, the observers, those who have never gone to work.

If you are tired of just drawing your breath and drawing your salary, if you are not content just to sit around and endure until you die, then here is good news: God has called you to serve Him, and He has *equipped* you to serve Him. He has given you a spiritual gift—something to discover, develop, and deploy for Jesus.

OCTOBER 4

About matters of the spirit: brothers,
I do not want you to be unaware.
1 Corinthians 12:1

When we talk about spiritual gifts, we are not referring to material gifts. We're talking about something much more valuable. Neither are we talking about natural gifts or talent. All talents are from God, but talents are not unique to the saved. Unsaved people are just as likely to be talented as Christians are.

Spiritual gifts are supernatural enablements given to God's children for service to Him. A spiritual gift may be *linked* to a natural talent, but it goes far beyond that. You may not realize it, but because of God's gifts, a Christian is someone who is naturally supernatural.

OCTOBER 5

You know how, when you were pagans, you were led to dumb idols—being led astray.

1 Corinthians 12:2

Just like it was in the Corinthian church, we still see people distorting the gifts of the Spirit. Someone will say, "Have you heard about the revival going on in thus and such a place? All kinds of strange things are happening. People are falling down like they're glued to the floor, some are indecently exposed, some are laughing out of control, some roaring like lions or barking like dogs."

The devil wants to give the Holy Spirit a bad name. He wants to take what is good and twist it, pervert it. He wants to make you think twice before embracing your spiritual gift.

OCTOBER 6

The prophets' spirits are
under the control of the prophets.
1 Corinthians 14:32

Let me tell you something about real revival. Real revival is never manifested by the gifts of the Spirit. Real revival is seen by the "fruit" of the Spirit—"love, joy, peace, patience, kindness, goodness, faith, gentleness, self-control" (Gal. 5:22–23). Real revival doesn't put you out of control; it puts you under the control of the Holy Spirit.

Sometimes people will say, "I was just carried away. I couldn't help it. God came over me, and I just had to to it." Not according to the verse above. As the Bible says, "Everything must be done decently and in order" (1 Cor. 14:40).

No one can say, "Jesus is Lord,"
except by the Holy Spirit.
1 Corinthians 12:3

Any time that worship draws you away from the Lord Jesus Christ—even worship that seems to magnify the Holy Spirit rather than the lordship of Jesus—that worship is contrary to the Bible. No one can say that Jesus is Lord but by the Holy Ghost.

You don't go beyond Jesus to the Holy Spirit. You may go *deeper* into Jesus, but you'll never go beyond Jesus. If you want to know whether any church or any music is Spirit-filled—if you want to know whether your spiritual gift is operating—ask this: "Is it giving preeminence to Jesus Christ?" That's all you need to know.

*There are different activities, but the same
God is active in everyone and everything.*
1 Corinthians 12:6

It's customary for couples to receive gifts when they get married. They are given waffle irons, blenders, toasters, can openers, coffeemakers. All these gifts have different functions, capacities, and applications, but if they use electrical power, they all have one thing in common—they have to be plugged in.

When the Bible talks about diversity of gifts, ministries, and activities, it just means they're different. They're not all the same. Yet God has given each one of these a provision, a purpose, and—most importantly—a power to enable it to operate. That power is the Holy Spirit.

Diligently keeping the unity of the Spirit
with the peace that binds us.
Ephesians 4:3

What is unity? It is not the same as *unison*. A choir sings in unity even while singing different parts. God doesn't want us all to be alike. We're not a congregation of clones. God makes us different that He might make us one in Him.

Unity is not *uniformity*. Uniformity comes from pressure from without. Unity comes from life from within. We all share the same Spirit.

Unity is not even *union*. We can all be members of the same church, but that doesn't make us united. Unity comes as we celebrate our different gifts, which all come from the same Spirit.

*A manifestation of the Spirit is given to each
person to produce what is beneficial.*

1 Corinthians 12:7

Your spiritual gift is not for your enjoyment; it
is for your employment. Your spiritual gift is a
tool, not a toy. It is to bless the church body.

God gives you a spiritual gift so that you might
do a job in and through the church. My gift is
going to bless you. Your gift is going to bless
me. We're going to bless one another. It's not an
introverted, self-centered gift. Spiritual gifts are
designed for mutual encouragement. It's not
"what's in it for me?"

Spiritual gifts are never an end in themselves.
They are meant to profit the entire body.

Based on the gift they have received,
everyone should use it to serve others.
1 Peter 4:10

My brown eyes are a natural characteristic that came to me when I was born. Spiritual gifts, however, are supernatural characteristics that come when we were born again. It is your joy and responsibility to discover and develop the gift that God has already given you.

Have you ever watched a baby discover his hands? He arrives with those hands, of course. You never go to the hospital and say, "Okay, it's time to put the hands on." No, he just shows up with those. But there comes a time when a child discovers his hands. Your spiritual gift is a birthday present like that. Learn to use it.

God also testified by signs and wonders . . .
and distributions of gifts from the Holy Spirit.
Hebrews 2:4

In the days ahead, we are going to look at the various gifts the Holy Spirit has distributed. There are two primary places in the Bible where spiritual gifts are listed: 1 Corinthians 12:8–10 and Romans 12:6–8. These passages are not an exhaustive listing of spiritual gifts, but they are illustrative and helpful.

I have broken the list into three categories:
• Teaching/Leadership Gifts
• Service Gifts
• Sign Gifts
To some degree these may seem arbitrary, but I believe it will give insight as we consider them.

When the leaders lead in Israel,
when the people volunteer, praise the Lord.
Judges 5:2

As we begin to look at the teaching/leadership gifts, it's important to note that these are the most practical and needed in the church, as well as the most common.

The first one we'll explore is leadership. This is not the motivation to be a big shot but rather the ability to coordinate things, to help people see the big vision, and to move them toward it for the glory of God. To be able to stand before others, coordinating and presiding over activities for a common goal, motivating people to see their place in the overall plan and direction, is a great need in the body of Christ.

The person who prophesies speaks to people for edification, encouragement, and consolation.
1 Corinthians 14:3

Prophecy is the ability to speak for God. It is not merely *foretelling* but *forthtelling*—speaking what God has said in His Word.

A lot of misinformation exists about prophecy. Some people today claim the role of prophet. But the Bible says that the church is "built on the foundation of the apostles and prophets" (Eph. 2:20), a foundation laid 2,000 years ago. You don't keep laying the foundation every story. You build on it. But although there is no more *office* of prophet, there remains the *gift* of prophecy—the ability to edify and build up, to exhort and fire up, to comfort and shore up.

*The Lord's slave must not quarrel,
but must be gentle to everyone, able to teach.*
2 Timothy 2:24

If you have the spiritual gift of teaching, you
have a desire to clarify truth. You have a hunger
for searching things out and for validating the
truth of messages that are presented. You have
a questioning mind that you feel compelled to
employ in Bible classes, neighborhood Bible
studies, backyard Bible schools, and other
venues where the Word of God is explored and
proclaimed.

You may use this gift as a mother, teaching your
children. You may use it as an instructor, opening up the Word for others to learn from and
understand. The church needs sound teachers.

*I found it necessary to write and
exhort you to contend for the faith.*
Jude 3

What is exhortation? It is the desire and ability
to stimulate people in their faith, to encourage
them to love Jesus more.

If you have this particular spiritual gift, you're
going to enjoy personal counseling, getting
involved with people who are struggling to
apply the truths of God's Word to their life and
its challenges. Perhaps you will be drawn toward
music ministry, where you can inspire people
through worship. You may also be valuable in
personal outreach and witnessing, going after
the lost, the straying, those far from home.
Thank God for the exhorters and encouragers.

My mouth speaks wisdom;
my heart's meditation brings understanding.
Psalm 49:3

What is wisdom, especially as it applies to the subject of spiritual gifts? It's not just a matter of being intelligent. It is not mere common sense. In fact, it is an uncommon sense.

Wisdom is the ability to see life from God's point of view. Certain people have this gift of godly wisdom. They're the kind of people you go to when you need guidance or insight on a certain matter or question. Those who have this gift make wonderful counselors, because they are enabled by God to take the lessons learned from the Word and from their own experience and apply it to your spiritual need.

*Do not believe every spirit, but test the spirits
to determine if they are from God.*
1 John 4:1

Another gift involves the discerning of spirits.
We need to learn that not everything spiritual
is of God. There is spiritual wickedness also,
and demons are masters of deception.

Because the devil has come up with so much
counterfeit flimflam, we desperately need those
in the church who have the spiritual ability to
discern spirits. This is not the ability to go
around judging everybody, trying to decide
who's saved and who's lost. We don't have the
prerogative to do that, as Matthew 7:1 warns.
But thank God for those who can pull away the
devil's cloak of deception.

*If anyone serves, his service should be
from the strength God provides.*
1 Peter 4:11

Now we begin looking at the various "service gifts," including the spiritual gift of ministry. This is another word for service. If this is your gift, you are going to find yourself meeting people's spiritual needs in a physical way.

Think of the great service that is performed for others through this gift in the church—those wonderful ushers, nursery workers, bus drivers, groundskeepers, maintenance staff, handymen, sound board operators, and numerous others who do the often unseen and unheralded tasks that make church life possible for everyone. They are God's army of ministering servants.

But who am I, and who are my people, that we
should be able to give as generously as this?
1 Chronicles 29:14

We are all commanded to give, knowing that
everything we possess is a gift from God, some
thing able to be shared generously with others.
But some people have the *gift* of giving.

These are especially motivated to entrust their
personal assets to others so that the work of
God may be carried on. They make good deci
sions in meeting others' immediate needs. They
don't just throw money around anywhere and
everywhere with no intended purpose, but they
are willing to give as God directs. They have
the ability both to accumulate and disperse.
They are spiritual givers.

*Think sensibly, as God has distributed
a measure of faith to each one.*
Romans 12:3

When Paul talks about faith here, he's not talk ing about the saving faith that is common to all Christians. He is speaking of superabundant faith—the *gift* of faith.

You read about this when Paul writes, "If I have all faith, so that I can move mountains, but do not have love, I am nothing" (1 Cor. 13:2). If God wants you to move mountains, He will give you mountain-moving faith. Not all of us have this kind of faith. But, oh, how I love to be around people who have great faith, who are enabled to trust Him for much and to inspire us all to greater hope and trust.

Your faith is great.
Let it be done for you as you want.
Matthew 15:28

George Mueller, who raised millions of dollars to feed orphans without ever asking for a dime, was once on borad a sailing ship, bound for an appointment in Newfoundland. Unexpectedly, the ship stopped in the ocean. Mueller asked the captain why. He answered, "We can't move because of the fog." Mueller said, "Well, I must not miss my speaking engagement. Let's go to the chartroom and pray that God will lift the fog." The captain went along to humor him. He saw Mueller drop to his knees and ask God for a miracle. When he rose to his feet, the fog had evaporated. Now, that's a gift some people have. Not everyone, but some of us.

Be merciful, just as your Father also is merciful.
Luke 6:36

Perhaps mercy is your spiritual gift. Oh, how needed this is! Mercy is the ability to identify with people and to comfort any of those who are in distress.

This is a gift that my wife, Joyce, certainly has. She is constantly reminding me about the needs of other people. That's because she has the gift of mercy. You have it too, if you feel sympathy and empathy for the misfortune and heartaches of others, if you mentally, emotionally, and practically relate to those needs. You will be drawn toward hospital visitation and benevolence ministries. These go with your gift.

*Though untrained in public speaking, I am
certainly not untrained in knowledge.*
2 Corinthians 11:6

"Sign gifts" are a third category of spiritual
gifts. And among these is the gift of knowledge.
This is the ability to know things that you
could not know other than by divine intuition
and revelation. It is not something that's learned
in school. It is God-given insight.

The devil counterfeits this gift (as he does all
the gifts). The counterfeit of this particular gift
is clairvoyance. Yet there is a spiritual gift of
knowledge whereby one can know things by
divine revelation that he could not know any
other way. Nobody knows everything, but some
do have a gift of knowledge.

To another, faith by the same Spirit,
to another, gifts of healing by the one Spirit.
1 Corinthians 12:9

Do I believe God heals? Absolutely. He heals by miracle and He heals by medicine and doctors. He heals instantaneously and He heals in time. And yes, there is a supernatural gift of healing, because the Bible includes it in its list. The gift of healing does not seem *normative* in this age, but I'd like to meet someone who has it.

If I did, I wouldn't put him up on stage somewhere to let selected people parade by him, but I would take him to the hospital, to the children's ward, and would look to see if he truly had the gift of healing. If God raises up someone today with this gift, I would rejoice.

John never did a sign, but everything
John said about this man was true.

John 10:41

Miracles normally came in clusters in the Bible. There were miracles, obviously, in the Creation, miracles around the ministries of Moses, Elijah, and Elisha, miracles with Jesus and the apostles, and there will be end-time miracles. I do not know anybody today who has the gift of miracles, but I would certainly not deny God's ability in that area. He's proven it too well.

However, I would rather have it said of me that many believed on Jesus through my word than that I had the power to do miracles—because that is the lasting miracle, the new birth, the greatest miracle of all.

I wish all of you spoke in other languages,
but even more that you prophesied.

1 Corinthians 14:5

What is the gift of tongues? It is the ability to speak in a language one has not learned. It is not an unknown language but a known one. The word translated as "tongue" is the Greek word *glossa*—"a recognizable language."

To have this gift is not a sign that one is Spirit-filled. As a matter of fact, tongues are not a sign to the saved but to the unsaved (1 Cor. 14:22). The sign that one is filled with the Spirit is not speaking in a tongue or language he does not know but controlling the one tongue he has. The primary purpose of this gift was to authen ticate the ministry and message of the apostles.

If there is no interpreter, that person should keep silent . . . and speak to himself and to God.
1 Corinthians 14:28

Everyone in the body is supposed to profit from the use of a gift. Suppose some foreign, unconverted Jews visited an early assembly of believers, and someone stood up and praised God in a language he had not learned but which these foreigners understood, since it was their native tongue. They'd be amazed . . . and convicted.

But what about the others in the church? They wouldn't understand the foreign language without an interpreter. There must then be someone with the gift of interpretation so all are edified and no one is left out. Tongues and interpretation must work together.

*I remind you to keep ablaze
the gift of God that is in you.*
2 Timothy 1:6

Finally, let's talk about *discovering* our gifts. First, it is a matter of lordship, of realizing that you are not your own. It is taking your hands off a gift that belongs to Him and has been given to you. You must sacrifice whatever keeps you from utilizing it.

Don't insult God by saying you don't have a grace gift. To deny your spiritual gift is not humility but unbelief and rebellion. To fail to use your gift for His body and His glory is a tragic waste. It is poor stewardship of the gift entrusted to you. One day you will answer to the Lord concerning how you have handled it.

*We who are many are one body in Christ and
individually members of one another.*
Romans 12:5

Here are four principles at work as we discover
our gifts within the context of the church:

1) *Enjoyment*—the liberating sense that you're
doing what feels natural.
2) *Encouragement*—being valued for the gifting
you bring to the body.
3) *Enablement*—the wonder of watching God
accomplish new things in you.
4) *Enlightenment*—the joy of cooperating with
the Lord as He empowers and instructs.

Get active in the church, and your spiritual gift
will begin to come to the surface.

Now you are the body of Christ,
and individual members of it.
1 Corinthians 12:27

Bill Gothard tells the illustration of a person at a party who spills a dessert tray. As people draw near to see what happened, the one with a gift of prophecy says, "That's what happens when you're not careful." The one with a gift of mercy says, "Don't feel bad; anybody could do that." The one with a gift of service says, "Hey, let me help you clean that up." The one with a gift of giving says, "I'll pay for a new dessert tray."

See how all the different gifts work together? God doesn't want you to go to church just to sit and soak. If you want to add meaning to life, discover your spiritual gift and put it to work.

November

How to Pray
with Power

Therefore, you should pray like this.
Matthew 6:9

In Matthew 6, our Lord showed us how to pray. Notice that He didn't say, "Pray this prayer." He said, "Pray like this." This is not a prayer to be repeated mindlessly.

Suppose we got together and you said to me, "Okay, say a conversation." That would be silly. Like conversation, prayer is not merely repeating words. It is talking with God. I confess there may be times when the words of this prayer fit my need perfectly. I may then want to repeat word-for-word what our Lord taught us. But I am not just mouthing words. I am praying out of my heart, using *His* words.

*If you believe, you will receive
whatever you ask for in prayer.*
Matthew 21:22

Many Christians would confess that the major failure in their life is not learning to pray well. That's because there is no sin in life that proper prayer could not help you avoid. There is no need in life that proper prayer could not supply. Nothing lies outside the reach of prayer except that which lies outside the will of God. What fools we are if we do not learn to pray!

So there is not a more important subject in all the world for a Christian—not only to learn *how* to pray, but how to pray with power. Prayer can do anything God can do, and God can do anything!

Father, Your name be honored as holy.
Luke 11:2

Who are the persons in this prayer? A child and his Father. We're coming to God and speaking to God as our Father. It's important to understand this, because real, powerful prayer—the kind that prevails—is for the children of God.

You might say this is to be taken for granted because everybody is a child of God. No, they're not. Jesus told the unsaved Pharisees, "You are of your father the Devil, and you want to carry out your father's desires" (John 8:44). The true children of God are "those who believe in His name" (John 1:12). Not everybody is a child of God—only believers!

You are all sons of God
through faith in Christ Jesus.
Galatians 3:26

Often we hear people speak of the universal fatherhood of God. But that is not right. All people are not necessarily brothers. We may be brothers in our humanity, but spiritually we are not brothers until we are born into the family of God and have one common Father.

The first thing that must occur if you want your prayers to be answered—if you want your prayers to be powerful—is to become a child of God. And in order to be a child of God, you must receive Jesus as your personal Savior. Have you done that? Does He live in your heart? If so, then you are ready to pray.

*Don't babble like the idolaters, since they
imagine they'll be heard for their many words.*
Matthew 6:7

You do not have to be an amateur Shakespeare
in order to pray. You do not have to pray in old
English or convoluted terms or poetic meter.
You can just talk to God out of your heart, the
way a child talks to his father.

Suppose when our children were at home, my
daughter had come to me and said, "Hail, thou
eminent pastor. I welcome thee home from thy
sojourn. Wouldest thou grant to thy child that
I may tread to the apothecary and procure some
cosmetics to adorn my face?" How absurd! We
just speak to God out of our hearts—not disre
spectfully, but with reverent familiarity.

*God has sent the Spirit of His Son
into our hearts, crying, "Abba, Father!"*
Galatians 4:6

Have you ever thought about calling the great God—the One who scooped out the seas and heaped up the mountains and flung the stars into place, who runs this mighty universe—have you ever thought about calling Him "Daddy"? Would that be irreverent?

No. God's Spirit in your heart cries out, "Abba, Father" if you have been born again. If you have taken your place in the family of God, you can spiritually crawl up into His lap, put your arms around His neck, and talk to Him as you would talk to your own Father. Your relationship with Him can be that intimate.

Pray to your Father who is in secret. And your
Father who sees in secret will reward you.
Matthew 6:6

Some people think you have to pray through a priest or a saint. They illustrate this by using the example of talking to the president. They say you would not go directly to the president; you would go through your senator or congressman, who would go to the president for you. They surmise from this scenario that you can't go directly to God but most approach Him by way of a go-between.

Well, I'm not going to my congressman if the president is my daddy. You can go directly to God your Father if you are born again by faith in the Lord Jesus.

Your kingdom come. Your will be done
on earth as it is in heaven.
Matthew 6:10

Prayer has one purpose and one purpose only. Its goal is that God's will be done. Prayer is not an exercise where we bend God's will and try to make it fit ours.

Too many people have the notion that prayer is how we make impassioned appeals in the hopes of talking God into doing something for us, even if it is something He would not ordinarily want to do. But this is not true.

Prayer is seeking the will of God and following it. Prayer is the way of getting God's will done on earth.

When You open Your hand,
they are satisfied with good things.

Psalm 104:28

When some people hear that the purpose of prayer is the will of God, they may say, "I knew there must be some catch to it. I don't want God's will if I don't get what I want." If you're thinking that way, let me tell you that God wants for you what you would want for yourself if you had enough sense to want it. God's will is best for you.

God loves you so much, and He gives all good things to those who walk uprightly in Him. Successful prayer is finding the will of God and getting in on it. You are not hemmed in by the will of God; rather, you are freed up by it.

*Whatever you ask in My name, I will do it so
that the Father may be glorified in the Son.*
John 14:13

While we know from His Word that certain things are the will of God, in other matters we must seek His will in prayer. Should you move to another city to take that new job? Should you sell your home? Which college should you go to? Who should you marry? But if we seek the will of God in all matters, we will come to know the will of God.

How? Jesus said, "If you remain in Me and My words remain in you, ask whatever you want and it will be done for you" (John 15:7). When we lean upon Jesus moment by moment, He will show us what to pray and how to pray.

*If you remain in Me and My words remain in
you, ask whatever you want and it will be done.*

John 15:7

It is the Holy Spirit within us who helps us to
pray. We pray *to* the Father, *through* the Son,
and *in* the Spirit.

If we surrender to the Spirit of God and abide
in Christ, then His Word abides in us. There
fore, we can pray for whatever we will. That's
because strangely and wonderfully, the things
we now desire are the same things He desires,
because we now have the mind of Christ oper
ating within us. As we pray, we are thinking the
thoughts of Christ after Him—loving what He
loves, hating what He hates. Our prayer begins
to line up in agreement with His will.

No one knows the concerns of God
except the Spirit of God.
1 Corinthians 2:11

One of the sweetest lessons I ever learned about prayer is this: the prayer that gets to heaven is the prayer that starts in heaven. Our job is just to close the circuit. God lays something on our hearts to pray for, we pray for it, and it goes right back to heaven.

Prayer is the Holy Spirit finding a desire in the heart of the Father, putting that desire into our hearts, then sending it back to heaven in the power of the cross. "Your kingdom come. Your will be done on earth as it is in heaven." We are to seek the will of God in all of our prayer, because that is the whole reason for doing it.

*My God will supply all your needs
according to His riches in glory in Christ Jesus.*
Philippians 4:19

This is one of the greatest verses in all the Bible. It does not say, "My God will supply all your wants," because there are times when we want things we do not need. There are also times when we need things we do not want.

But God will supply all our "needs"—not *out of* His riches, but "according to" His riches. A millionaire may give you ten dollars *out of* His riches, but that's not necessarily in *accordance to* His riches, in the same manner as His riches, in relation to His riches. When we ask for God to meet our needs, He meets them with an abun dant measure of supply.

Give us today our daily bread.
Matthew 6:11

This verse does not imply that all we can ask for is bread. We have many needs. That's the reason I was careful to point out to you that this is not a prayer to be mechanically repeated. It is a model prayer.

If you need bread, ask God for bread. If you need a job, ask God for a job. If you need a house, ask God for a house. Let the Holy Spirit show you what you need to ask for, then pray in the Spirit that your needs will be met. God wants to meet your needs, but you cheat yourself by failing to pray. "You do not have because you do not ask" (James 4:2).

Give me neither poverty nor wealth;
feed me with the food I need.

Proverbs 30:8

I was a young pastor in Florida, still in college. And one day, as I was preparing to return to school, a deacon arrived at my house with two big canvas bags of oranges. "Adrian," he said, "I can't eat all these before they spoil. Take them back to college with you and give them away."

The next day, I saw a little boy come and steal an orange from one of the sour orange trees that grew in my yard. But had he just come to the door and asked, I would have loaded him down with oranges he could actually eat. That's what happens when we do not ask, when we think we know what's best for us.

The sacrifice of the wicked is detestable to the Lord, but the prayer of the upright is His delight.
Proverbs 15:8

Sometimes prayer is not answered because we are not praying to God as a Father. We have never been saved.

Sometimes prayer is not answered because we are not praying in the will of God. We're saying, "*My* kingdom come. *My* will be done."

Sometimes prayer is not answered because we have unconfessed, unrepented sin in our lives.

And sometimes prayer is not answered because we just don't pray. Change these things about your praying, and you'll see a big difference.

If I had been aware of malice in my heart,
the Lord would not have listened.

Psalm 66:18

Scripture does not say that if you have sinned,
the Lord will not hear you. If that were the case,
He would not hear any of us. God has only said
that He will not hear when we know about sin
in our life and refuse to do anything about it.

"Indeed, the Lord's hand is not too short to
save, and His ear is not too deaf to hear. But
your iniquities have built barriers between you
and your God, and your sins have made Him
hide His face from you so that He does not
listen" (Isa. 59:1–2). It's not that He can't hear.
Our active, unconfessed sins come between us
and a holy God.

*Anyone who turns his ear away from hearing
the law—even his prayer is detestable.*

Proverbs 28:9

Let's suppose you are like the average Christian
and say, "Nobody's perfect. Everybody has sin
in his life." A grudge, an attitude, a habit. Just
a little pet sin.

Now let's say you come to God to pray for your
sick child, asking Him to make her well. Do
you think God is going to hear your prayer?
No, He won't! It's not just that you have sinned
against Him in the past but that you are aware
of active sin now. So if He did what you were
asking of Him, He would actually be encourag
ing you to sin. You must deal with your sin first
by owning up to it and asking His forgiveness.

*Forgive us our debts, as we also
have forgiven our debtors.*

Matthew 6:12

I can't repeat this point enough, because it is
where so many people struggle: if you are pray
ing with unrepented sin in your life, you are
wasting your breath! Your prayers are getting
no higher than the ceiling lights.

Also remember that God chooses to forgive us
in the manner that we forgive others. If you say
of someone, "I'm not going to forgive him,"
God says, "Then I'm not going to forgive you."
If you say, "Okay, I'll forgive her, but I won't
have any more to do with her," He will say,
"Okay, I'll forgive you, but I won't have any
more to do with you." That's just the deal.

God doesn't listen to sinners, but if anyone is God-fearing and does His will, He listens to him.

John 9:31

I heard about a little girl who was angry with her mother. Early one night, her mom put her to bed and told her to say her prayers before she went to sleep. The little girl got down on her knees and prayed for her brother, sister, daddy, aunts, uncles, and everybody—"Amen." Then she looked up at her mother and said, "I guess you noticed you weren't in it." That is not the kind of prayer that gets answered.

Is there unconfessed sin in your life right now? It may be big; it may be small. But if so, don't be surprised if God is not hearing your prayer. He loves the prayers of His obedient followers.

Do not bring us into temptation,
but deliver us from the evil one.
Matthew 6:13

There is a devil. He is very real. And he wants to keep you from praying.

He says to his demons, "Keep that person from talking with God, because if you can keep him from communicating with his Father, we can beat him every time. But if he prays, he will beat *us* every time."

It has been said that the devil trembles when ever he sees even the weakest saint upon his knees. And so, my friend, we need to pray, "Do not bring us into temptation, but deliver us from the evil one."

*The Lord knows how to rescue
the godly from trials.*
2 Peter 2:9

The phrase "Do not bring us into temptation" may be translated, "Lead us lest we fall into temptation." We need to pray daily that the Lord would deliver us.

Have you ever committed a sin, asked God to forgive you, and He did? Now let me ask you another question: After you asked God to forgive you for that sin, did you commit that same sin again—even after God had forgiven you? And have you repeated that sin as many as ten times or more, having to come back to God and say, "It's me. I did it again"? Does He continue to forgive? Yes, if we're sincere.

Keep Your servant from willful sins;
do not let them rule over me.

Psalm 19:13

Don't you get tired of coming back to God with the same old sins to confess, begging for mercy for this one repetitive transgression? Why do you keep having to do this? It's probably because you have understood the phrase "Forgive us our debts" but not the phrase "Do not bring us into temptation."

The first part is the *pardon* of the Lord's Prayer. The second is the *protection* of it. The reason we have to come back to God so many times asking forgiveness is that we have not put on His protection that would keep us from falling so repeatedly.

*The Lord is faithful; He will strengthen
and guard you from the evil one.*

2 Thessalonians 3:3

Many of us jump out of bed in the morning feeling pretty good. We do not sense any real need for prayer. The sun is shining brightly. We have our breakfast, drink our coffee, and sail out of the house into the day. But at some point the unexpected happens. We have a head-on collision with Satan, and we fall. He knows how to ensnare us. We pray, "God, I'm so sorry! Please forgive me."

However, this is not a prayer to be prayed at the end of the day but at the beginning. This prayer is not the latch that closes the door at night. It is the key that opens the door in the morning.

The one who lives under the protection of the Most High dwells in the shadow of the Almighty.

Psalm 91:1

When we wake up, we must put on the armor of our Lord Jesus Christ and make no provision for the flesh. We must immerse ourselves in the presence and power of God. Then God builds a wall of fire around us as we say, "Dear Lord, deliver us from the evil one. Lead us lest we fall into temptation."

We tend to think we are capable of handling it ourselves. We think we can go through the day and overcome the devil in our own strength. Prayerlessness and pride always go together. But it's time to pray for protection—to get off the defensive and go on the offensive.

Do not be conquered by evil,
but conquer evil with good.

Romans 12:21

I have a friend, Mike, who was a linebacker for the Miami Dolphins. I remember hearing him tell about a time when his coach asked him to do some scouting for him. "What kind of play ers are you looking for, coach?" he asked. The coach answered, "You know the kind of guy who gets knocked down and keeps getting up?" Mike said, "Is that the guy you want?" The coach replied, "No, I want to find the guy who's knocking everybody down."

It's one thing to bounce back from a fall. But wouldn't you like to be one who resists the devil and makes him flee from you?

Give the Lord the glory due His name;
worship the Lord in the splendor of His holiness.
Psalm 29:2

Notice that the Lord's Prayer both begins and ends with praise. "Our Father in heaven, Your name be honored as holy," and, "Yours is the kingdom and the power and the glory forever." All powerful prayer is packed with praise.

Why? Because praise is an expression of faith. Prayer is faith turned inside out. Faith is what causes our prayers to be answered.

When we pray in the will of God with clean hearts, we can expect God to answer us. And if we have difficulty with our praying, it may be because we are not praising Him enough.

I will praise You forever
for what You have done.
Psalm 52:9

When we bring our petitions before God, we enter His presence in order to take something away. But when we praise Him, we enter His presence in order to stay there forever.

This pleases the Lord. It blesses Him when we offer up the sacrifice of praise, because "He is your praise and He is your God, who has done for you these great and awesome works your eyes have seen" (Deut. 10:21).

The most powerful prayers are always filled with worship, knowing that He is "enthroned" on the praises of His people" (Ps. 22:3).

The man of God replied, "The Lord is able to give you much more than this."
2 Chronicles 25:9

When I got ready to go away to college, my dad said to me, "Son, I wish I could pay your way to school. I'm not able to, you know, but I sure would like to." That always meant a lot to me.

I'm glad, though, that my heavenly Father will never say to me, "Son, I'd like to, but I can't." Our heavenly Father is the King of kings. We have the heart of the Father and the hand of the King. We have a Father who can hear us and a king who can answer us. Therefore, we should always pray earnestly, fervently, expectantly, and praisefully unto Him, because He is both willing and able.

*He split rocks in the wilderness
and gave them drink as abundant as the depths.*

Psalm 78:15

I was talking to a young boy who said, "God has called me to preach, and He wants me to go to school, but I don't have any money. So I don't guess I can go." I said, "If I could get a millionaire to help you, would you go?" His eyes lit up and he said, "I sure would!" I said, "Well, you have the One who owns the world—Almighty God. If God can't do it, who can?"

Where God guides, He provides. He may use a millionaire or some other means, but His is the kingdom, the power, and the glory. What a great God we pray to! And what fools we are if we don't.

December

HOW TO UNDERSTAND
THE BIBLE

Open my eyes so that I may see
wonderful things in Your law.
Psalm 119:18

I want you to learn how to study your Bible, to make it burst aflame in your hand. Knowledge is power in any realm, whether business, athletics, or theology. But nowhere is it more true than in relation to the Word of God.

A Kenyan believer once wrote, "Lord, from the cowardice that dares not face new truth, from the laziness that is contented with half-truth, from the arrogance which thinks it has all truth—good Lord, deliver me." I hope you'll not have cowardice, laziness, or arrogance as you approach the Bible, because it is truth—God's truth—that transforms.

For as he thinks within himself, so he is.
Proverbs 23:7

I heard about a sign that read, "We are not what we think we are; what we think, we are." That's right. We truly are what we think.

So since it's true that knowledge carries so much power, we need the knowledge of the Word of God in order to have spiritual power. We need to be molded, motivated, and managed by the Word of God. And yet for many people, the Bible remains a closed, mysterious book. They really don't understand it, even though they could if they wanted to. While there's no lazy, magical way to understand it, it is not impossible. In fact, it is joyful and thrilling.

*I will praise You with a sincere heart
when I learn Your righteous judgments.*
Psalm 119:7

Psalm 119 is by far the longest psalm in the Bible. In it, the psalm writer gives us a number of statements about the Word of God. In fact, nearly every one of its 176 verses makes some mention of the "ordinances," the "statutes," the "judgments," the "precepts," the "decrees," the "commandments" of God.

As you read this chapter from the Bible—and as we go through the final month of our time together—make note of three things:
• Appreciate the virtues of the Word of God
• Assimilate the vitality of the Word of God
• Appropriate the values of the Word of God

*The entirety of Your word is truth,
and all Your righteous judgments endure forever.*

Psalm 119:160

One of the greatest virtues of the Scripture is that it is timeless.

Psalm 119:89 says, "Lord, Your word is forever; it is firmly fixed in heaven." Psalm 119:152 says, "Long ago I learned from Your decrees that You have established them forever."

Forever! Other books may come and go, but the Bible is here to stay. Thousands of years have passed since it was written. Empires have risen and fallen. Civilizations have come and gone. Science has pushed back the frontiers of human knowledge. And yet the Bible still stands.

DECEMBER 5

*The ordinances of the Lord are reliable
and altogether righteous.*

Psalm 19:9

Dr. Robert G. Lee had this to say about the Bible: "All of its enemies have not torn one hole in its holy vesture, nor stolen one flower from its wonderful garden, nor diluted one drop of honey from its abundant hive, nor broken one string on its thousand-stringed harp, nor drowned one sweet word in infidel ink."

Emperors have decreed its extermination, and atheists have railed against it. Agnostics have cynically sneered at it, and liberals have moved heaven and earth to remove the miracles from it. Materialists have ignored it, but the Bible stands—timeless, ultimate, indestructible.

Your righteousness is an everlasting righteousness,
and Your instruction is true.

Psalm 119:142

Not only is the Bible timeless and "everlasting," it is also reliable and truthful. Psalm 119:151 says, "You are near, Lord, and all Your commands are true." All of them!

In the Gospel of John, Pilate asked Jesus, "What is truth?" (John 18:38). Jesus had already answered that question in John 17:17 when, speaking to His Father, He said, "Your word is truth."

In a world that has lost its appreciation for truth in a sea of relativism, you can say without stutter or stammer that the Bible is truth.

Truth has gone from My mouth,
a word that will not be revoked.
Isaiah 45:23

Today there are all kinds of attacks on the truth of the Bible. There's the frontal attack from liberals who deny the truth of the Bible. But there's also an attack from the rear, which is perhaps even more insidious. These are not the people who deny the truth of the Bible. These are people who put their own experience over the Word of God.

They say, "I know what I feel and what I think." Sometimes they'll even argue, "I don't care what the Bible says. Let me just tell you what I've experienced." But experiences are not a reliable source of truth. Only God's Word is truth.

*If anyone thinks he is a prophet or spiritual,
he should recognize . . . the Lord's command.*

1 Corinthians 14:37

Paul dealt with some people in Corinth who
had let experience trump the truth of God's
Word. Apparently, some of those in the church
had ventured into charismatic hocus-pocus,
going wild about tongues, prophecies, visions,
and ecstasies. Paul tried to set them in order,
but they said things like, "Let me tell you,
Brother Paul, what a spiritual man I am. Why,
I have the gift of prophecy."

Paul said, "Well, if you think you have the gift
of prophecy, you'll know that what I'm telling
you is the Word of God." It is the Bible, not
experience, that is the benchmark of truth.

Whatever was written before
was written for our instruction.

Romans 15:4

In addition to the frontal attack against the Bible from those who deny it, and in addition to the rear attack by those who substitute their experience for the Word of God, there is an attack from the flank by people who want to replace it or prop it up with psychology, philosophy, and other things—as if the Bible is not good enough on its own.

But, friend, the Bible is true. If you're looking for truth, you can be sure to find it there. As it says in 2 Timothy 3:16, the Bible is inspired—"God-breathed"—verifying its authority in the trustworthy name of God.

*Man must not live on bread alone but on every
word that comes from the mouth of God.*
Matthew 4:4

God did not breathe into the Scriptures. He
breathed the Scriptures out. Yes, He used men
like Isaiah, Jeremiah, Matthew, Mark, and Paul,
but these men just held the pen of God. They
were the voice of God as God was speaking.

If you read the Old Testament, you will find
phrases like "the Word of the Lord" or "the
Word of God" or "God spoke" or "the Lord
said" used 3,808 times. If the Bible is not the
Word of God, it's the biggest bundle of lies that
has ever come to planet Earth. The Bible is
truth—the absolute truth—because the God
of truth cannot speak error.

*Instruction from Your lips is better for me
than thousands of gold and silver pieces.*
Psalm 119:72

Is this verse true of you? Is the Bible worth
more than "gold and silver" in your estimation?
If you were to ask me to choose between a huge
stack of gold, silver, rubies, diamonds, stocks,
and bonds on the one hand, and the Word of
God on the other, I would not hesitate for even
a moment. I would choose the Word of God
over every possible possession known to man.

The Bible should be a treasured book. Psalm
119:127 says, "I love Your commandments
more than gold, even the purest gold." Or as
verse 103 says, "How sweet Your word is to my
taste—sweeter than honey to my mouth."

Whoever keeps His word,
truly in him the love of God is perfected.
1 John 2:5

The saints and the heroes of our faith have pillowed their heads on the Word of God as they walked through the chilly waters of the river of death. The martyrs who died for the witness of Jesus Christ have held the Bible to their bosoms as the creeping flames lapped around their feet. The members of the early church, persecuted and outcast by society, loved the Word of God. They never questioned it, and they argued little about it. They preached it, pronounced it, and poured it forth like white-hot lava. They loved it, lived it, practiced it, trusted it, and obeyed it. May our testimony about the Word of God be the same.

DECEMBER 13

*By knowledge the rooms are filled
with every precious and beautiful treasure.*
Proverbs 24:4

Do you know why the Bible is treasured? You've known the answer for a long time—"Jesus loves me, this I know, for the Bible tells me so." That's it. You will never have a victorious Christian life if you do not love this book.

The Bible is like a treasure. Suppose there was buried treasure in your backyard. You'd go down to the hardware store and get a spade, if you didn't already have one. In the same way, the Bible is worth mining and discovering when we find ourselves near it. It is a timeless book, a truthful book. For all these reasons and more, it should also be a treasured book.

The words that I have spoken to you
are spirit and are life.
John 6:63

The Bible is a living book. It possesses vitality. As Hebrews 4:12 says, "The word of God is living and effective and sharper than any two-edged sword, penetrating as far as to divide soul, spirit, joints, and marrow; it is a judge of the ideas and thoughts of the heart."

But even though the Bible pulsates with life, it doesn't come to life in *you* until you assimilate it. You don't just read a cookbook, for example. You use its instructions to prepare a meal to eat. Likewise, no matter how much you may appreciate the Word of God, what good does it do you unless you assimilate it?

*May He incline our hearts toward Him to walk
in all His ways and to keep His commands.*
1 Kings 8:58

Several things will happen to you as you begin
to assimilate the Word of God. First, your eyes
will be opened. You may have 20/20 vision, but
God has to open your eyes in order for you to
behold the wondrous things contained in the
Scriptures.

Not only will your *eyes* be opened, however;
your heart will be stirred. If you don't have a
desire for the Word of God right now, instead
of feeling guilty or spiritually inferior, just pray
to the Lord and say, "Please incline my heart to
Your Word. Move in my life, open my eyes,
and stir my heart to seek Your will and ways."

DECEMBER 16

*Then He opened their minds
to understand the Scriptures.*
Luke 24:45

Once your eyes are opened and your heart is stirred by claiming and embracing the Word of God, your mind is going to be enlightened. Psalm 119:73 says, "Your hands made me and formed me; give me understanding so that I can learn Your commands."

How often in my sermon preparations have I put down my pencil and bowed my head to say, "O, my God, help me to understand this. Lord, give me Your understanding." When we pray like this, our hearts are moved and our minds are enlightened to grasp, apply, and understand the Word of God.

I rise before dawn and cry out for help;
I put my hope in Your word.

Psalm 119:147

It takes time to ponder the Word of God. So if you have to rise an hour early, do it. If you have to stay up an hour late, do it. Do whatever it takes so that you will have time to ponder what God says to you in the Bible.

I suggest, too, that as you ponder the Word of God, you should keep a pad and pencil handy. I almost invariably read the Bible with a pen or pencil in my hand. Why? Because I'm expecting to receive something. If you're not doing that, it tells me you're really not expecting God to do anything as you're reading and studying His Word.

*Happy is a man who finds wisdom
and who acquires understanding.*
Proverbs 3:13

When you read the Bible, use your sanctified common sense. Don't just jump into the middle of a chapter or book with no plan about what you're doing. The Bible is like any other book in that it contains a number of different forms of speech. You see poetry as poetry, prophecy as prophecy, precept as precept, promise as promise, proverb as proverb.

If you try to turn the proverbs into promises, you'll lose your religion. The proverbs are not promises. You read them with a different set of eyes and ears. Bible study—like anything else worthwhile—is deliberate and purposeful.

Think about Him in all your ways,
and He will guide you on the right paths.

Proverbs 3:6

The book of Proverbs talks about ways to be healthy, wealthy, and wise. But you can do all those things and be hit by a truck. Then you're not very healthy anymore, and you're certainly not wealthy. If you'd been wise, you would have looked both ways. The proverbs are good, but don't try to turn them into promises.

So as you look at the Bible, consider what you are reading. Ask yourself, "Is this a precept? A prophecy? Poetry? Prose? Proverb? Promise?" God gave you a mind, but He doesn't just zap you with knowledge. Remember, you have the mind of Christ. Use it.

This is a symbol for the present time.
Hebrews 9:9

Sometimes people ask, "Is the Bible supposed to be interpreted literally or figuratively?" The answer is, "Yes." The Bible is to be interpreted literally and figuratively all at the same time.

In the book of Revelation, for example, the devil is described as a huge dragon with a tail so long that he sweeps a third of the stars from heaven. Today, we know about stars that are billions of light-years into outer space. Could there be a dragon whose tail is big enough to wipe out that many stars? This passage is talk ing about the devil and the fallen angels. See, it's symbolism, but it has a literal application.

The law has only a shadow of the good things to come, and not the actual form of those realities.

Hebrews 10:1

When you're driving down the highway and you spot yellow arches on a sign near a particular building, you know that you're approaching McDonalds. But when you see those yellow arches, do you say, "Oh, that's just a symbol. There's not really any such thing as a fast-food restaurant that sells hamburgers"? Of course not. The arches are a symbol of a reality. You find out what the symbol stands for, and then you literally apply it.

The same thing goes for interpreting the Bible. Yes, there is a lot of symbolism in the Scripture, but the symbols point to actual realities.

How I love Your teaching!
It is my meditation all day long.
Psalm 119:97

Here are six age-old questions to ask when you are studying the Bible:

1) Is there a promise to claim?
2) Is there a lesson to learn?
3) Is there a blessing to enjoy?
4) Is there a command to obey?
5) Is there a sin to avoid?
6) Is there a new thought to carry with me?

These are great starter questions whenever you are preparing a Sunday school lesson or Bible study. Take any passage of Scripture, ask these questions, and you've got your lesson!

*I have treasured Your word in my heart
so that I may not sin against You.*
Psalm 119:11

After you pray over and ponder the Word of God, you need to preserve the Word of God. That means you hide His Word in your heart.

You may not realize or believe this, but you can remember far more than you think you can. In fact, we function by memory. Your mind is a marvel. And even though we all tend to be a little more forgetful as we age, our memories remain a powerful tool in helping us navigate life—especially when we have preserved the Word of God in them. As Psalm 119:16 says, "I will delight in Your statutes; I will not forget Your word."

The prophets become only wind,
for the Lord's word is not in them.
Jeremiah 5:13

My wife enjoys collecting pretty little boxes. Sometimes, since other people know about her affinity for these containers and decorations, friends and family members will bring boxes to her from other countries. Some of the little boxes in her collection are intricately carved or covered with diamonds. You might see one and say, "What a marvelous little box that is." But do know what you would find if you looked inside it? Probably paper clips, rubber bands, toothpicks, or an old breath mint.

Your mind is a lot like those boxes. They can be pretty outside, but still be full of junk inside.

Their life will be like an irrigated garden,
and they will no longer grow weak from hunger.
Jeremiah 31:12

Yesterday I compared your mind to one of Joyce's ornamental boxes—pretty, but full of ordinary, everyday, incidental things.

Your mind could also be compared to a garden. Have you noticed how much easier it is to grow weeds than flowers and vegetables? When Adam fell, his mind became a garden of weeds. Ours will do the same thing if left untended. So in order for your mind to preserve the Word of God, you have to cultivate it. You have to weed your garden. Fill your mind with the Word of God, so that what is inside will flow forth with blessing and honor to God.

*How happy are those whose way is blameless,
who live according to the law of the Lord!*
Psalm 119:1

I love the first few verses of confidence and challenge that follow the one at the top of this page. "Happy are those who keep His decrees and seek Him with all their heart. They do nothing wrong; they follow His ways. You have commanded that Your precepts be diligently kept. If only my ways were committed to keeping Your statutes!" (Ps. 119:2–5).

It is not enough to recite the promises without obeying the commandments. Do you want to learn more about the Word of God? Then obey the part you already know. "For whoever has, more will be given to him" (Matt. 13:12).

DECEMBER 27

Walk in His ways, keep His statutes,
commands, and ordinances, and obey Him.
Deuteronomy 26:17

The more you obey the Word of God, the more you will learn of it. As Mark Twain was reported to have said, "It's not the part of the Bible I *don't* understand that gives me so much trouble. It's the part I *do* understand."

Yes, there may be mysteries and other things you don't understand, like the third toe on the left foot of a beast in Revelation. But I will tell you one thing you *can* understand: "Love one another." When the Bible gives you such a clear command, do you live based on the knowledge it gives you? Keep the things you do understand, and the Word will become real to you.

*I will speak of Your glorious splendor
and Your wonderful works.*
Psalm 145:5

Listen to some of these verses from Psalm 119:

• "With my lips I proclaim all the judgments from Your mouth" (Ps. 119:13).
• "Help me understand the meaning of Your precepts so that I can meditate on Your wonders" (Ps. 119:27).
• "I will speak of Your decrees before kings and not be ashamed" (Ps. 119:46).

Let the Word of God be constantly in your mouth. Stow it in your heart, show it your life, and sow it in the world. The more of it you give away, the more of it will stick with you.

I pursue the way of Your commands,
for You broaden my understanding.
Psalm 119:32

A person might come to me and say, "I'm just so weak, I can hardly get out of bed. I don't feel good enough to do anything." I might say, "Well, have you been to the doctor?" If the person says no, I might ask, "Do you think you have a disease? What are you eating?"

Suppose he said, "There's a restaurant I go to on Sunday. I get a meal there if it's not raining. That's all I ever eat." Well, *of course*, he's weak. Friend, a sermon on Sunday is designed to whet your appetite, not to feed you for a solid week. The Word of God is your source of growth. Stay in it, and you'll start to feel stronger.

Your statutes are the theme of my song
during my earthly life.
Psalm 119:54

The Word of God is a source of victory. Just as Jesus appropriated the Scripture to overcome Satan in the wilderness, you can use it to help you overcome your own temptations.

The Word of God is also a lasting source of joy. Psalm 119:111 says, "I have Your decrees as a heritage forever; indeed, they are the joy of my heart."

Likewise, the Word of God is a source of power. The psalmist said in Psalm 119:28, "I am weary from grief; strengthen me through Your word." The Word of God will strengthen you.

*Your word is a lamp for my feet
and a light on my path.*
Psalm 119:105

When we spend time studying and meditating on the Word of God, we are able to find our way. It may be dark, but His Word will illuminate the path beneath us if we trust Him.

Do you want guidance? Do you want victory? Do you want growth? Do you want joy? Do you want power? Then, friend, look no further than the Word of God to supply you with all these blessings. You can appropriate them, but only after you assimilate them. And you can assimilate them only if you appreciate them. I promise that if you do all these things, the Word of God will transform your life.